The NESA
Activities Handbook
for Native and
Multicultural Classrooms

Volume Three

The NESA
Activities Handbook
for Native and
Multicultural Classrooms

Volume Three

Compiled by
Don Sawyer and
Wayne Lundeberg

TILLACUM LIBRARY
Vancouver, Canada

THE NESA ACTIVITIES HANDBOOK FOR NATIVE AND
MULTICULTURAL CLASSROOMS, VOLUME THREE
Copyright © 1993 Native Education Services Associates

TILLACUM LIBRARY
A Division of Arsenal Pulp Press
100-1062 Homer Street
Vancouver, B.C. Canada V6B 2W9

The publisher gratefully acknowledges the assistance of the
Canada Council and the Cultural Services Branch, B.C.
Ministry of Tourism and Ministry Responsible for Culture.

Typeset by the Vancouver Desktop Publishing Centre
Printed and bound in Canada by Kromar Printing

CANADIAN CATALOGUING IN PUBLICATION DATA:

Main entry under title:

The NESA activities handbook for native and
    multicultural classrooms, volume three

ISBN 0-88978-263-6

   1. Indians of North America—Education.
2.Minorities—Education.   3. Experience.
I.Sawyer, Don, 1947–   II. Lundeberg, Wayne, 1951-
III. Native Education Services Associates.
E96.2.N47 1993   371.97'97   C93-091859-2

CONTENTS

Introduction 7

Getting Comfortable 12

Multicultural Bingo 15

Acknowledging Positive Qualities 19

Mind Map 23

Painting The Circle 26

Values Auction 29

Take a Stand: An Exercise in Values 39

Storytelling 43

Creating a Group Culture 46

The Mystery Culture 51

Causes Of Racism 59

Faces: An Exercise in Preconceptions 64

World Mapping 68

World Web 72

Views of Man and Nature 74

Families 83

Gender and Work 86

Characteristics of a Native Community 89

The Shihiya Case Study 99

Mapping Traditional Territories 111

The Newcomers 114

Behaviours That Impede
Native/Non-Native Relationships 121

Community Futures 126

Thanks to the Centre for Curriculum and Professional Development, B.C. Ministry of Advanced Education, Training and Technology, for permission to include "Characteristics of a Native Community," "The Shihiya Case Study," "Mind Map," and "Acknowledging Positive Qualities."

The script for "The Mystery Culture" is adapted from "The Albatross" by Theodore Gochenour in *Beyond Experience: The experential approach to cross-cultural education.* eds. Donald Batchelder and Elizabeth G. Warner. Experiment in International Living Press in co-operation with SIETAR International, 1977. Used with permission.

"Childhood in an Indian Village" by Wilfred Pelletier in "Characteristics of a Native Community" used with permission.

The editors wish to thank all those who gave permission for their materials to be included in this collection. Every attempt was made to contact copyright holders of the materials included in the handbook; further information pertaining to the rights of any of these materials would be welcome.

INTRODUCTION

This third volume of activities is a response to the continuing demand for effective, experience-based exercises appropriate for Native and multicultural learning situations. The first two volumes in this series of activity guides have gone into multiple printings, and response to the ideas and structured experiences provided has been overwhelmingly positive. We have been gratified by the steady increase in interest in these handbooks since the first volume was published in 1984.

The continued popularity of the first two volumes of *The NESA Activities Handbook for Native and Multicultural Classrooms* is the result of an increased sensitivity to the need to accommodate and address cultural differences, and to develop an appreciation in learners of all ages for the sense of 'otherness' in those around them. The key to a better and more equitable society lies in valuing and appreciating these differences. The growing recognition of the effectiveness of experiential, co-operative education has contributed to the acceptance and broad use of the techniques presented in the handbooks. From primary teachers to adult education instructors, educators are discovering an appreciation for techniques that provide and expand on concrete experience. They see the value of activities that encourage critical thinking, genuine dialogue, and mutual respect, and they recognize the importance of meaningful experiences that can be used to develop a variety of language, thinking, and interpersonal skills while increasing knowledge and furthering an understanding of concepts.

Recent events have underscored the need for non-Native Canadians to better understand the realities of Native conditions and aspirations and their historical roots. It is equally important that Native students see their community and reality reflected in the educational programs in which they participate. The activities collected here attempt to develop an attitude of respectful inquiry and understanding toward all cultural and ethnic groups while concentrating on creating a dialogue around Native issues.

While nearly half of the activities in this volume focus on Native peoples, we have attempted to provide a broader multicultural orientation to make the collection useful in a wider variety of situations. This broader orientation recognizes that the issues raised have a place in all classrooms, whether the learners are primarily Native or not. Developing an awareness of and appreciation for cultural and socio-historical differences is critical to us all.

It is also important to note that even the Native-oriented activities do not have to be used only in Native classrooms or in Native studies programs. Many of them can be used as case studies for examining the larger issues of colonialism, multiculturalism, ethnocentrism, cultural relativity, and the socio-historical roots of contemporary situations. Some can be adapted for application to other minority groups.

This third volume shares many of the characteristics with our first two sets of exercises: the activities represent a range of structured experiences, are specially designed to focus on both Native and multicultural issues, and encourage experiential learning. This collection, like the first, contains both original and borrowed exercises. Many of the original activities were drawn from a variety of curriculum projects designed for use at all levels, especially secondary and adult. Whether original or adapted, all activities were selected for their effectiveness in bringing important cross-cultural issues into the classroom.

Having pointed out that the activities are usable in a variety of classroom situations, it should also be noted that the exercises are loosely organized into multicultural and Native sections, with the first activities being more multiculturally-oriented and those toward the end having a more specific Native focus.

The activities included represent a range of what has come to be known as structured experiences. Structured experiences, as defined by Pfeiffer and Jones (1979), are "designed for experience-based learning and not merely for fun," though participants often thoroughly enjoy them. Consensus exercises, simulation games, clarification activities, and group process exercises are all represented in this collection. Though the activities vary in type and objective, they all provide opportunity for significant experiential learning.

The effectiveness of experiential learning lies in its directness. What is learned emerges directively and inductively from the experience. Unlike conventional teaching, which is mediated and generally based on lecturing, reading and recitation, the experiential model doesn't rely on indirect or vicarious learning. The concreteness of the experience and the immersion of the participants in it give students a base from which to extend inquiry and to apply what is learned to their lives.

John Dewey (1963) noted that all genuine education comes about through experience, but he was quick to point out that not all experience is of equal educational value. The determining factor is the quality of the experience. Dewey said that there must be two dimensions to an experience for it to be genuinely educational: it must be enjoyable and engage the learners, and it must "live fruitfully and creatively in subsequent experiences." That is, it must have some lasting and positive impact. Our task as educators, he states, is to provide experiences that meet these two criteria.

Structured experiences both involve students and provide the experiential base for significant personal growth and learning. Properly used, and this often means in conjunction with more conventional approaches, structured experiences can produce significant and predictable learning outcomes. Boocock and Schild (1981) conclude that "simulation games are not just a refreshment from 'real' learning, not just a special method for handling those students for whom little learning is expected, but have a direct impact on intellectual learning, attitudes and strategies."

They go on to point out that these activities have been shown to appeal to and be effective with both the achieving and non-achieving student. Games and activities provide an impetus for students frustrated with school, at any point, to become actively involved. Furthermore, because participation depends on factors other than straight academic skills, students from a broad academic background can participate together, developing greater acceptance and understanding.

A further finding—that knowledge which results from games and activities has little correlation with conventional classroom learning (Boocock and Schild, 1981)—suggests that experiential exercises do more than replicate conventional learning. Instead, they provide a way of teaching concepts, skills, and attitudes which is often ignored by traditional techniques. Perhaps of greater importance are the kinds of issues which can be raised through the use of structured experiences. Such difficult concepts as values, identity, community structure, culture and cultural differences, prejudice, power and powerlessness, and social stratification, can be dealt with honestly and effectively in the classroom. Experiential exercises can lead to considerable self- and social-awareness and can have significant impact on attitudes. They can become the basis for future actions.

Each activity includes a section called "Notes on Use." This is an attempt to share with facilitators the experiences we have had conducting the exercise. The comments included are general observations about problems and opportunities to watch for, hints for operating the game more smoothly, and ideas for utilizing the activity to its full potential.

Another section that should be noted is the final portion of each activity, "Debriefing." Educators working with experiential activities generally concur that the key to making these experiences maximally effective is the debriefing, or follow-up. During this portion of the exercise the facilitator has the opportunity to help learners to extrapolate from the exercise, to gain additional meaning, and to apply the learning that has resulted to their own lives.

Pfeiffer and Jones (1979) outline a five-step cycle for administering and debriefing structured experiences. The first phase, experiencing, is the activity phase when the game or exercise is actually conducted. Following this is the publishing or sharing phase when participants discuss their reactions and observations. Next is the processing stage when general patterns are established and discussed. Generalizing—developing principles and linkages with the real world—follows. Finally, participants reach the applying stage where they see the relevance of the experience to their own lives and develop strategies for applying it.

The debriefing sections in this handbook primarily contain specific questions that can be used to structure the discussion. More general suggestions for ways of approaching the debriefing phase are also offered, but neither is intended to be definitive. We encourage you to develop your own questions and approaches that work for you.

Finally, we urge you to view these activities as starter ideas. We hope that you will find them useful and effective, but we also hope that you will adjust and modify them to better accommodate your needs and the needs of your students. Better yet, develop your own activities to fit your situation. We'd be delighted to hear your comments or ideas regarding the material in this book, and we encourage you to send us any new activities you may have developed.

We trust that you will find, as we have, that these activities help create more exciting and vital classrooms where relevant and meaningful learning occurs.

References

Boocock, Sarane and Schild, E.O., eds. *Simulation Games in Learning.* Beverly Hills: Sage Publications, 1981.

Dewey, John. *Experience and Education.* New York: Collier Books, 1963.

Pfeiffer, J. William and Jones, John, eds. *A Handbook of Structured Experiences for Human Relations Training*, Volumes I-IX. San Diego: University Associates, 1979-1985.

GETTING COMFORTABLE

Purpose

To help participants identify what they need to feel comfortable before participating in structured experiences, and to use these expressed needs to ensure the creation and maintenance of a safe environment.

Time Required: 30 to 45 minutes.

Materials: Flip chart or chalkboard.

Notes on Use

Many structured experiences require ways of participating and levels of disclosure with which some participants may not be familiar or comfortable. This activity acknowledges this and allows students to discuss their concerns and establish a 'safe' environment for participation. You may wish to use this as an initial exercise to introduce the concept of safety generally or as a way of leading into one or more structured activities. Begin with a clear description of what will be expected of participants. How long you give to this process—or even if you use it at all—will be determined by the experience of the participants, the nature of the unit and activities you are teaching, the level of disclosure that will be required, and the responses of the individuals.

Although you must be willing to address each concern, the main purpose is to create an atmosphere of acknowledgement and honesty rather than to solve all problems; most participants will feel more comfortable and willing to participate if they feel they have been heard. Much of this is consensus building: this is what I need from you; what do you need from me and the rest of the participants? In extreme cases, you may have to provide students who cannot feel safe with an opportunity to opt out. If a good environment has been created, if the fun and excitement of experiential learning has been emphasized and explained, and if the facilitator is open and sensitive, this is rarely necessary.

Procedure

1. Begin by explaining what activities you have planned and how they fit into the unit you are presenting. Emphasize the experiential nature of the activities and why they have been chosen, and that while they should be fun and interesting, they may also be somewhat demanding. (For an explanation of experiential learning, see the NESA introduction.) Lay out carefully and fully what your expectations are of the participants (such as full participation, genuine sharing of ideas, openness to the ideas of others, willingness to take some risks).

2. Have students list for themselves their individual needs with regard to each activity, class, or seminar. After they have thought about this issue and completed their lists, have them volunteer items they have identified. List these on the board or flip chart. Items such as confidentiality, trust, humour, patience, support, etc., may be identified.

3. Discuss with the group whether their needs are currently being met within the group. If the participant(s) do not feel they are, explore what is required. Outline what you will do to establish the required circumstances for general participation. This might mean some icebreaker activities, discussing confidentiality and getting a general commitment to keeping personal disclosures within the group, talking about being supportive of one another, etc.

4. After the concerns have been discussed and steps to address those concerns outlined, ask for a general com-

mitment (this could take the form of a group contract) to participate in the activities and to honour any agreements which have been negotiated in order to create an atmosphere of safety.

Debriefing

Discuss the importance of feeling safe in a group. Explore experiences where members did and did not feel safe in a group and how those experiences felt. Ask students if this activity has helped allay their fears and whether they are clearer on what is expected of them by the group and the facilitator. End by emphasizing the group bonding that has taken place and the new level of confidence and safety that has resulted.

MULTICULTURAL BINGO

Purpose

To act as an 'icebreaker' for new groups and to illustrate the impact of Canada's multicultural society on individual members.

Time Required: 20 to 30 minutes.

Materials: Copies of the bingo card for each participant.

Notes on Use

This is a fun and interesting way for participants in new groups to get to know one another. If the facilitator knows some details about the participants in advance, the bingo cards can be more specific; if the group is unknown to the facilitator, the cards tend to be more general in content.

The example given focuses on multicultural information. A blank bingo card is provided so the facilitator can make up cards appropriate for any specific group.

Procedure

1. Begin by composing an appropriate bingo card for the group.

2. Hand out the cards and explain that it is up to the participants to question one another to find people who fit the descriptions on the cards and to collect their autographs. The first person who gets five autographs in a row (or a blackout) is the winner.

3. Start the bingo session and mingle with the participants,

encouraging them to talk with as many group members as possible. Everyone must continue until they have five autographs in a row, even after someone has won.

Debriefing

What did participants discover about their fellow group members? Were they surprised?

Do you feel more comfortable with one another after the activity? Why is it important in a group to feel that you know your fellow participants? What role does trust play in groups? What helps to build trust?

BINGO

Find someone who:

Sample Bingo card

BINGO

Find someone who:

knows what Ramadan is	was born outside of Canada	likes sushi	knows in which country Tagalog is an official language	has seen a foreign film this year
has attended a wedding ceremony of a different culture	has relatives who live in a place with civil unrest	can speak a language other than English	knows when Chinese New Years is this year	has visited more than five countries
has been south of the equator	has been to a mosque	knows a refugee	has been to an Indian Reserve in Canada	lives in an extended family
can cook Mexican food	knows who Krishna is	has attended ethnic celebrations in Canada	has lived in another country	has visited Quebec
is wearing clothing made in Asia	ate something today which came from a foreign country	has been to a Jewish Passover dinner	has a spouse from another cultural group	owns a Japanese car

ACKNOWLEDGING POSITIVE QUALITIES

Purpose

To contribute to students' positive self-image through a process of sharing self-identified qualities and positive feedback with a partner.

Time Required: 45 to 60 minutes.

Materials: Instruction Sheets 1 (About Yourself), and 2 (About Your Partner), for each participant.

Notes on Use

This activity asks students to look at things they like about themselves as well as things they like about their partners. At the beginning of the activity, acknowledge that this process may sometimes be difficult; you might want to ask participants if they feel uncomfortable discussing positive things about themselves and why. Explain the importance of being able to identify and acknowledge our strengths as well as our weaknesses. You may wish to have students pair up or to place them together to develop stronger interpersonal relations. Occasionally students with stronger self-concepts work well with those less confident. Some students may have difficulty with the activity: be patient and provide support and encouragement as needed. The items on the instruction sheets are suggestions: modify as appropriate for your group.

Procedure

1. Advise students that this activity asks them to focus on their own positive characteristics and those of others in the group. Ask them to think about what they like about themselves and others in the class.

2. Pair students with a partner and have them sit across from each other.

3. Hand out Instruction Sheet 1: About Yourself. Tell the participants that they have 15 minutes to complete the tasks outlined on the sheet, and remind them to alternate answering. If they finish early, ask them to discuss how they felt during the exercise.

4. After 15 minutes, hand out Instruction Sheet 2: About Your Partner. Participants again have 15 minutes to work through the tasks outlined on the instruction sheet.

5. Time may be provided for students to write about their feelings or memories before debriefing.

Debriefing

Discuss the importance of acknowledging and celebrating positive traits, talents and achievements of both ourselves and others.

How did you feel when you had to reveal positive qualities about yourself? How did it feel when you pointed out good points in your partner? Why was this easier? How did it feel when your partner provided positive comments about you? Why?

INSTRUCTION SHEET 1:
ABOUT YOURSELF

Take turns telling your partner the following things one at a time:

1. Two physical qualities you like about yourself.
2. Three personality characteristics you like in yourself.
3. One talent or skill you have that you like.
4. Your two most satisfying achievements.
5. Your two most meaningful or happy relationships.
6. A dream you have for yourself where you are at your best.

INSTRUCTION SHEET 2:
ABOUT YOUR PARTNER

Take turns telling your partner the following things one at a time:

1. One physical feature your partner has that you really like.

2. One personality characteristic your partner has that you really like.

3. One talent or skill your partner has that you really like.

4. A vision you have of your partner being at his or her best: Where? Doing what?

5. One positive thing that you are feeling towards your partner right now.

MIND MAP

Purpose

To make a diagram of values, experiences, and influences which are important to students, and to reflect on and discuss these issues. For participants to note similarities and differences among the group.

Time Required: 30 minutes to 1 hour.

Materials: Enough sheets of chart paper and felt pens for each participant.

Notes on Use

This simple activity can help students to reflect on their past and future, and allows for a student-directed discussion of values and influences. It provides an opportunity for students to introduce aspects of family and their past, as well as hopes for the future, and can thus be an effective introductory activity or icebreaker. The activity can be done with $8\frac{1}{2}$" by 11" sheets of plain paper and fine markers or pencils, but the chart paper is more effective and provides a more easily shared map if participants will be presenting to a larger group. Note that this can be a high-risk activity for some participants. You may prefer to use it as an introductory exercise after some trust and rapport has been established within the group.

Procedure

1. Distribute felt pens and chart paper to each participant.
2. List possible mind mapping topics on the board or flip

chart. Emphasize that these are simply suggestions: students may use any categories they wish. Suggested general topics: family, hobbies, community, work, school, commitments, future goals, major experiences, values and beliefs, cultural/ethnic background.

3. Instruct each student to complete a cluster with his or her name in the centre. Lines extending from the centre are labeled with the category title and lead to specific information about the individual. You may wish to make a sample map, such as the one that follows, and show it to the group as an example.

4. When students are finished, have them share their maps in small groups, explaining and elaborating as they wish. If the exercise is being used as a general introductory activity, this might be followed or replaced by a sharing of the maps with the group as a whole.

Debriefing

Acknowledge the diversity of the group, the richness of experience within the group, and the range of interesting backgrounds, as well as the common factors and issues.

Was it difficult to chart yourself? To share with others? Did you find the range of experiences and background interesting? Surprising? What do you know about the group now that you didn't before?

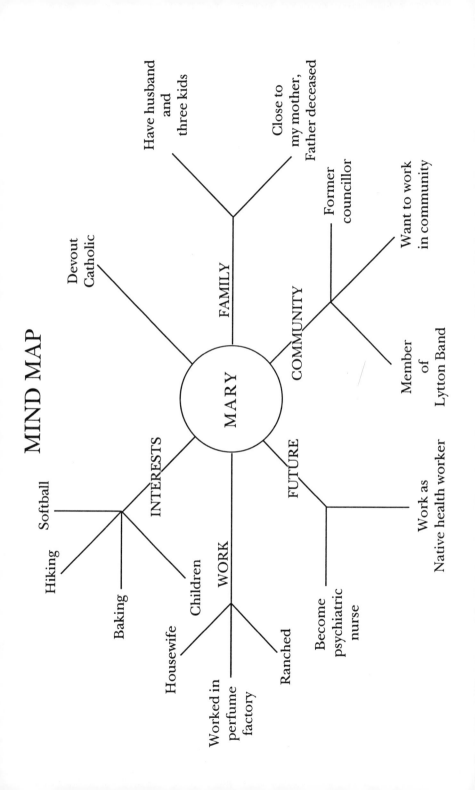

MIND MAP

MARY

FAMILY
- Have husband and three kids
- Close to my mother, Father deceased

Devout Catholic

COMMUNITY
- Former councillor
- Want to work in community
- Member of Lytton Band

INTERESTS
- Hiking
- Softball
- Baking
- Children

WORK
- Housewife
- Worked in perfume factory
- Ranched

FUTURE
- Become psychiatric nurse
- Work as Native health worker

PAINTING THE CIRCLE

Purpose

To build inclusion through a co-operative, non-verbal group exercise and provide a basis for examining feelings related to group process.

Time Required: 1 hour.

Materials: Enough long or circular tables (or use the floor) to accommodate as many groups of 5 to 8 students as are in the class, an assortment of poster paints, enough brushes for each participant, a sheet of flip chart paper for each participant, taped music.

Notes on Use

This activity can generate feelings of initial uncertainty, but usually culminates in a sense of group camaraderie as students, who start by painting their own picture, end up contributing to the completion of several. Set-up is the most demanding aspect for the facilitator. Make sure you have plenty of paint in a variety of colours (markers can be substituted but are not as effective), probably three or four jars for each two paintings, and have paper for each participant set out in a circle so the participants can easily circulate from painting to painting. Provide space for the paintings to be posted.

As the participants paint, play taped music to create a mood. You may wish to change the music or put together a tape that has a variety of music to explore how the different styles and tempos affect the composition. You can allow participants to establish their own groups, or you may wish to form groups intentionally to develop co-operative relations among diverse students.

Procedure

1. Set up tables with 5 to 8 (depending on size of group, age, and time available) sheets of poster paper and adequate brushes and paints.

2. Explain to students that they will be participating in an activity that involves them interpreting the music through their painting, and that they will be asked to rotate to the painting on their right on a signal from the facilitator. They are then to continue the painting already in progress. Ask students to be aware of their feelings during the activity.

3. Instruct students to choose a piece of paper and stand in front of it.

4. Begin playing the music and ask students to begin painting once they have a feel for the music. Allow them to paint for about 2 to 3 minutes, then call out 'change.' Students move to their right and add on to the next painting. Proceed like this until all students have had a chance to add to all paintings.

5. When all paintings are done, turn off the music and have students post the paintings around the room, then debrief.

Debriefing

Begin by asking students what their predominant feelings were as they began. As they first moved to another painting? As they moved to the fourth or fifth painting?

If your feelings changed, why? Were there moments of fear, hesitation? How did you overcome them? What was happening in the group that was helpful? What did you find difficult? How did the music affect your painting?

Shift to the finished paintings. Does each have a theme? How did the paintings evolve? How are they different from the first painter's original idea? Are the initiators satisfied? What has been learned about group process from the activity?

VALUES AUCTION

Purpose

To have learners reflect on values that are important to them and test these experientially. To develop greater personal clarification of beliefs and values and provide a basis for discussing these concepts at an individual and cultural level.

Time Required: 1 to 2 hours.

Materials: Copy of 'Values and Needs That Are Important to You,' 'Auction Bidding Form,' and keys for each student.

Notes on Use

This activity has proven to work well with a variety of age and cultural groups. Besides helping students clarify what is really important to them, the exercise also allows the facilitator to look at values cross-culturally, and to determine whether some cultural groups place more worth on certain values than others. Although the three phases of the activity—initial ranking, budgeting and bidding, and evaluation based on the key—may seem a little complicated, together they result in a thorough, fun exploration of personal and cultural values. Some of the terms and concepts may seem abstract and unfamiliar to younger students, so be prepared to discuss and explain so that everyone is comfortable with them. The auction is the heart of the game: the facilitator should try to simulate the excitement and tension of a real auction as much as possible.

Procedure

1. Explain that you are going to explore values—things that are important to each of us. Then hand out copies of 'Values and Needs That Are Important to You' to each student. Instruct them to go through the 17 items and rank them according to importance in the left-hand space provided: A for extremely important, B for quite important, C for moderately important, and D for not important. Explain the concepts whenever necessary.

2. Have students go through the 17 items again and rank them in order of importance from 1 to 17: 1 for most important, 2 for second most important, and so on.

3. Hand out copies of the 'Auction Bidding Form' to students. They have exactly $1,000 each to spend during the auction. They should go through the 34 items up for sale and, keeping in mind that they have only $1,000 to spend, they must decide on how much they are willing to bid on each item. These amounts go in the first column. Some explanation of vocabulary and concepts may be necessary.

4. After students have budgeted for each item, begin the auction. As the auctioneer, keep the bidding going and have fun with the role. On the 'Auction Bidding Form,' students should write the highest amount they bid on an item in the second column, *even if they did not win it.* After each item is sold, the winning bidder should mark an X in the right-hand column and subtract what he or she paid from his or her total. Continue this process until all items have been sold.

5. Allow students to talk about the auction and how it felt. (Did they bid higher on some items than they had budgeted? Why?) Hand out copies of the key. Explain that the items that were auctioned correspond to the values that they have already rated. Have them study the key, noting

those items they bid high on, and especially those that they won. What values did their bidding suggest were *really* important to them? Finally, students should compare their bidding results with their original rankings on the 'Values and Needs That Are Important to You' handout. How are the corresponding items similar? Different? Why?

Debriefing

Since this exercise deals with values, some strong feelings may be evoked. Do students feel the results were accurate? Were they surprised by the results? Do they have a better idea of what is really important to them?

How do people develop their values? How have they developed the values that they hold? How do our values affect the way we live our lives?

For a cross-cultural perspective, discuss how values are imbedded in cultures and are informally transmitted from generation to generation. Break students into groups along cultural lines and ask them to compare results from the auction. Instruct them to record items and corresponding values on which individuals in the group tended to bid high. Have each group present their results.

Are there similarities? Are there significant differences? If there are cultural patterns, discuss why this might be. What do the patterns suggest about the cultures? If no patterns emerged, why? Would there have been clearer patterns 200 years ago? How would the responses of each group have been similar to or different from those 200 years ago? Why? How do cultures change? What aspects are most persistent and resistant to change?

VALUES AND NEEDS
THAT ARE IMPORTANT TO YOU

The following is a list of values and needs that may or may not be significant in your life. Please mark each item with a *letter* and a *number*.

First, consider each item individually. Grade each as A, B, C, or D to indicate whether you consider it extremely important (A), quite important (B), moderately important (C), or not important (D). Write these in the first column.

Then, consider all the items together. Number these values and needs according to their importance in your own life: 1 for the most important, 2 for the second most important, and so on. Write these in the second column.

___ ___ **Justice**　　　The quality of being impartial or fair; righteousness; conformity to truth, fact, or reason; to treat others fairly or adequately.

___ ___ **Altruism**　　　Regard for or devotion to the interests of others.

___ ___ **Recognition**　Being made to feel significant and important; being given special notice or attention.

___ ___ **Achievement** Accomplishment; a result brought about by resolve, persistence, or endeavour.

___ ___ **Pleasure**　　　The agreeable emotion accompanying the possession or expectation of what is good or greatly desired. 'Pleasure' stresses satisfaction or gratification rather than visible happiness; a state of gratification.

___ ___ **Wisdom**　　　The ability to discern inner qualities and relationships; insight, good sense, judgment.

___ ___ **Honesty** Fairness or straightforwardness of conduct; integrity; uprightness of character or action.

___ ___ **Autonomy** The ability to be a self-determining individual.

___ ___ **Wealth** Abundance of valuable material possessions or resources; affluence.

___ ___ **Power** Possession of control, authority or influence over others.

___ ___ **Love** Affection based on admiration, benevolence; warm attachment, enthusiasm or devotion; unselfish devotion that freely accepts.

___ ___ **Aesthetics** The appreciation and enjoyment of beauty for beauty's sake.

___ ___ **Physical Appearance** Concern for the beauty of one's own body.

___ ___ **Health** The condition of being sound in body; freedom from physical disease or pain; the general condition of the body; well-being.

___ ___ **Emotional Well-Being** Freedom from overwhelming anxieties and barriers to effective functioning; a peace of mind; inner security.

___ ___ **Knowledge** The seeking of truth, information, or principles for the satisfaction of curiosity, for use, or for the power of knowing.

___ ___ **Religious Faith** Communion with, obedience to and activity on behalf of a supreme being.

AUCTION BIDDING FORM

Items to be Auctioned	Amount Budgeted	Highest Amount Bid	Items Won
1. A chance to rid the world of prejudice.	_____	_____	_____
2. A chance to serve the sick and needy.	_____	_____	_____
3. A chance to become a famous figure (movie star, baseball hero, astronaut, etc.).	_____	_____	_____
4. A chance to complete a project in the field of your choice, to be widely recognized and acclaimed.	_____	_____	_____
5. A year of daily massage and the world's finest cuisine from the world's best chef.	_____	_____	_____
6. A chance to know the meaning of life.	_____	_____	_____
7. A vaccine to make all persons incapable of graft or lying.	_____	_____	_____
8. A chance to set your own working conditions.	_____	_____	_____

9. A chance to become the
   richest person in the
   world.   _____   _____   _____

10. A chance to become the
    Prime Minister of Canada.   _____   _____   _____

11. The perfect love affair.   _____   _____   _____

12. A house overlooking the
    most beautiful view in the
    world, in which you may
    keep for one year 40 of
    your favourite works of
    art.   _____   _____   _____

13. A chance to become the
    most attractive person in
    the world.   _____   _____   _____

14. A chance to live to age
    100 without illness.   _____   _____   _____

15. Free psychoanalysis with a
    genius analyst.   _____   _____   _____

16. A complete facsimile of a
    major public library for
    your private use.   _____   _____   _____

17. An audience with the
    leader of your faith.   _____   _____   _____

18. A chance to rid the world
    of unfairness.   _____   _____   _____

19. A chance to donate $1 million to charity. _____ _____ _____

20. A chance to be voted Outstanding Person of the Year and praised in every newspaper in the world. _____ _____ _____

21. A chance to master the profession of your choice. _____ _____ _____

22. A year with nothing to do but enjoy yourself, with all needs and desires automatically met. _____ _____ _____

23. A chance to be the wisest person in the world, and to make only right decisions for one year. _____ _____ _____

24. A chance to sneak 'authenticity serum' into every water supply in the world. _____ _____ _____

25. A chance to do your own thing, without hassle. _____ _____ _____

26. A room full of pennies. _____ _____ _____

27. A chance to control the destinies of 500,000 people. _____ _____ _____

28. The love and admiration of the entire world. _____ _____ _____

29. Unlimited travel and tickets to attend any concert, play, opera or ballet for one year. _____ _____ _____

30. A Total Makeover: new hairstyle, new wardrobe from the designer of your choice, and two weeks at an exclusive beauty spa. _____ _____ _____

31. Membership in a great health club. _____ _____ _____

32. An anti-hangup pill. _____ _____ _____

33. An omniscient computer, for any and all facts you may need. _____ _____ _____

34. A chance to spend six months with the greatest religious figure of your faith, past or present. _____ _____ _____

KEY: THE AUCTION TECHNIQUE

The items featured in the auction correspond with values and needs already studied:

Auction Items	Values and Needs
1 and 18	Justice
2 and 19	Altruism
3 and 20	Recognition
4 and 21	Achievement
5 and 22	Pleasure
6 and 23	Wisdom
7 and 24	Honesty
8 and 25	Autonomy
9 and 26	Wealth
10 and 27	Power
11 and 28	Love
12 and 29	Aesthetics
13 and 30	Physical Appearance
14 and 31	Health
15 and 32	Emotional Well-Being
16 and 33	Knowledge
17 and 34	Religious Faith

TAKE A STAND:
AN EXERCISE IN VALUES

Purpose

To encourage participants to explore their values through physical activity. To explore an active and interesting technique which can be used in various situations.

Time Required: 30 minutes.

Materials: A list of Values Questions for the facilitator.

Notes on Use

The single most important rule for the facilitator is to make participants take a stand on the issues. It is also important to keep the pace of the activity fast. Allow the participants to quickly say why they made the choice that they did, but do not let the discussion bog down with the 'what ifs', the 'buts', and the many different shades of grey that any of these issues have in real life. This exercise is a good energizer and is easy to use on the spur of the moment. Different statements can be developed for different purposes: development issues, immigration policies, multiculturalism, etc.

Procedure

1. Introduce the activity and make it clear to participants that they must choose one answer or the other: there can be no middle ground.

2. Gather the participants in the corner of the room after

they have cleared enough space to move freely from one side to the other. Explain that you are going to read through a list of questions with two options, (a) and (b). Option (a) will be assigned one side of the room and option (b) the other side. Participants must choose the option with which they agree the most and physically move themselves to the side of the room assigned to that option.

3. Read through the questions one by one, slowly and clearly. After each question, the participants must quickly make their decision and go to the appropriate side of the room. Ask some participants from each side of the room at random why they chose their option. Keep the comments brief and fast-paced. Do not allow the discussion to bog down. Not every participant need explain his or her choice on each question, but each person should be called upon at some point to offer their reasons for their choice.

4. After the questions are finished, instruct participants to return to their places, and debrief the activity.

Debriefing

Were your choices influenced by your cultural backgrounds? Could any of the choices linked to culture cause conflict with the values of the dominant culture? (such as extended families, parental influence, etc.)

Are there any right or wrong values? What can be done to help defuse conflicts based on cultural values?

TAKE A STAND
VALUES QUESTIONS

NOTE: These questions are suggestions only and should be modified and adapted to be relevant to individual groups.

1. In a confrontational situation in a group, it is better to:

    (a) compromise to retain group unity.
    (b) stand up for your principles.

2. The most important thing for a woman is to:

    (a) always give priority to her children's wellbeing.
    (b) put her own wants and needs first.

3. It is more important for a country to have:

    (a) military security.
    (b) an extensive social welfare system.

4. If our parents give us advice that we do not agree with, we should:

    (a) follow their advice.
    (b) do what we think is right.

5. It is more important to:

    (a) have a prestigious, well-paid job.
    (b) do something we enjoy.

6. The most important thing is:

    (a) family unity.
    (b) the happiness of the individual.

7. It is more important to:

   (a) conform to society's norms.
   (b) be oneself.

8. It is more important to get:

   (a) a formal university education.
   (b) experience in the real world.

9. It is more important to have:

   (a) the recognition of others.
   (b) a sense of personal achievement.

10. People are happier:

   (a) in an extended family, with several generations in one house.
   (b) in a nuclear family, with parent(s) and children only in the house.

STORYTELLING

Purpose

To examine the role of traditional stories in passing on the values of a culture.

Time Required: 1 to 2 hours.

Materials: No special materials are needed.

Notes on Use

This activity is best used in multicultural groups where a variety of traditional stories is likely to be identified, but it may also be used to good effect in more homogeneous groups. In the version presented here, the focus is on traditional stories such as fairy tales or folk tales, but the facilitator may allow participants to identify any story from their youth that they feel had a lasting impact on them, whether they are from movies, cartoons, children's books, etc.

Procedure

1. Introduce the concept of traditional stories, such as fairy tales, folk tales, myths, etc. Traditional stories function as lessons which are passed down from one generation to the next, carrying the values and histories of a culture. Ask participants to take a few minutes to think of a favourite story from their childhood and to try to remember the story in as much detail as possible.

2. Have participants form small groups of 4 to 6 people and share with one another their recollections of the stories they have chosen. Because individuals may remember

details differently or put a different emphasis on the story, permit participants to tell their story in full, even if others in the group are familiar with it. Encourage the participants to be as expressive and dramatic as possible to make the story come alive. You may wish to demonstrate with a story of your own before the students begin. The participants should try to identify what it was about their story which led them to choose it.

3. After all the participants in a group have had a chance to tell their stories, instruct the group as a whole to try to identify the underlying truths of the stories, and the messages which they implied (e.g., values such as truth, honesty, selflessness; good triumphing over evil; roles in society, in the family, of men and women). They should attempt to identify recurring themes or symbols which are in more than one of the stories.

4. Have the groups prepare a presentation of their discussions to share with the larger group.

Debriefing

Did you find it difficult to identify a suitable story? How comfortable were you with the messages and lessons of the traditional stories? Were there any dramatically opposing messages in the stories? Which stories are relevant and meaningful for living in our society today? Try to summarize common values and themes which seemed to recur.

How many chose religious stories? Why is it that we often perceive our own religious stories as 'truth', but relegate the religious stories of others to 'myth'? Do you feel that religious stories still have valid lessons for today's multicultural society?

What is the main source of traditional stories in our modern society? (TV, movies, books?) Are people happy with the messages and values that children are receiving today? Do we have any way of controlling or modifying the messages our children are exposed to?

How important is it for individual cultures to maintain the stories, beliefs and values that are unique to their culture? What stories and mythologies could help shape a tolerant, multicultural society?

CREATING A
GROUP CULTURE

Purpose

To examine the most fundamental aspects of culture—beliefs and values—and explore these by developing a common set of 'cultural' parameters and experiencing some of the subtle conflicts that can occur when people with different culturally-based beliefs interact.

Time Required: 1½ to 2 hours.

Materials: Pencil and paper for each participant, flip chart paper for each group, 3" by 5" adhesive labels for each participant, broad and fine markers—one colour for each group.

Notes on Use

This activity could be used after the concept of culture has been introduced and discussed, as a follow-up to distinguishing between material and non-material culture (see *NESA Activities Volume Two*) or it may be a lead-in to an examination of culture with a more sophisticated group. You may want to set the activity up by first discussing what culture is and is not, brainstorming aspects of culture and categorizing them as material and non-material, and establishing that the heart of a culture is contained in its non-material dimension—its values and beliefs.

Some participants, especially younger students, may have

difficulty coming up with a list of personal beliefs. This is often because they are not clear about the definition of a belief or value. Emphasize that these are principles that people try to live by. They are *not* interests (e.g. swimming, Nintendo). If students are really stuck, you might ask them what they would most like to see happen in the future. You may get comments like "world peace" or "a cleaner environment." Point out that these, then, are values and principles the individual believes in. On the other hand you might get a general response like "a better world." In this case ask the student to be more specific—what would make the world a better place?

The value of the activity depends on each group coming up with a strong set of common beliefs, and being willing to struggle to arrive at them. In the process some individual beliefs and values will have to be shelved—individual differences can be tolerated but do not define the group. Help individuals get away from arguing for their personal beliefs in favour of working collaboratively toward finding a common set of values they *can* agree on. This may require compromise and good interpersonal skills. Also, the more diverse the groups' lists of values, the better. To facilitate this, you may wish to group participants according to common attributes (e.g. religion, culture/race, gender).

If a group reaches an impasse and it appears they may be unable to arrive at a common list, work with them to identify values that may not have been considered and might thus be less contentious. It is critical that each group arrive at a list of common values.

During the mixing session, make sure all participants are involved. Encourage them to circulate as much as possible. Also ensure that all interactions are preceded by appropriate handshakes and greetings, but stress that these are only preliminaries—the focus of the encounters should be on discussing the different values on the participants' tags. Although the second mixer is not necessary, it allows participants to re-establish their group ties and to reinforce their distinct identity. It also gives them the opportunity to explore the in-group/out-group experience in more depth and to become familiar with the activity's format and rules.

Procedure

1. Have participants begin by listing beliefs and values that are important to them. You may wish to explain that values and beliefs in this context are principles that participants hold most strongly, beliefs that they try to live by and from which they will probably never budge. Encourage participants to look at genuine, personal values, principles they really embrace, not broad universals they feel they *should* embrace. Avoid giving any more examples than necessary, but encourage participants to be as specific as possible (e.g.: "Don't just say 'love'; make sure you say love for what or whom.").

2. When participants have completed their personal list, instruct them to prioritize these in terms of importance to them.

3. Form participants into groups of 4 or 5. Instruct groups that they are to arrive at 5 values that each member of the group strongly supports. There must be *full consensus* on each belief decided upon. These are to be based on individual lists, but are not limited to them. Provide a time limit for this phase: depending on the group, from 10 to 15 minutes.

4. As the groups decide on their common beliefs and values, have one of the members write them on a piece of flip chart paper.

5. After groups have reached consensus on their 5 items, have them design a crest or symbol that represents their group, their 'culture.' The symbol might have some relationship to one or more of the values upon which the

group has decided. Place the symbol on the flip chart with their values/beliefs.

6. Have participants put their symbol on the adhesive labels and list the 5 values/beliefs they have agreed upon. The tag must be clearly visible to others.

7. Have the group members develop a special handshake that is used only by their group members, and instruct them to decide upon an oral greeting to use when meeting each other or members of other groups. This could be a word or two or just sounds. Again, the greeting might relate to the values and beliefs already arrived at.

8. Now instruct participants that they will be joining with the other groups in a general mixer. They will be expected to shake hands (using their own special handshake and greeting) when they approach a new participant. They can speak in pairs or threesomes, but each participant must shake hands and greet each other before beginning speaking. After the greetings, they are to study the tags on the visitors they are speaking with and talk about their values. They are to listen politely, but their main aim is to explain their own values and attitudes and convince the newcomer that their beliefs are correct. They are encouraged to speak with as many members of other groups as possible.

9. First general mixer: 10 minutes.

10. After the conclusion of this session, have participants return to their own groups and greet each other appropriately. They are then to discuss the mixing experience. They may wish to share impressions of the other groups, discuss other groups' lists of values, or develop strategies for explaining their values. Allow about 5 to 10 minutes for this discussion.

11. (Optional) Second general mixer: 10 minutes (See Notes on Use).

12. Return to groups for debriefing.

Debriefing

Focus on the initial phase of arriving at a set of common beliefs and attitudes. Was it difficult to arrive at a personal list? Why or why not? How about a group list? How closely did the final group list look like your personal list? Why?

What was the biggest obstacle to arriving at consensus? How was this overcome?

How is this process similar to experiences you have had in real life? Did you feel more a part of the group after reaching and charting a common set of values? After putting on a tag with them listed on it? Why?

Discuss the mixing sessions. How did it feel when shaking hands with someone from another group? What handshake did you finally use? How did it feel to hear their greeting? How did you feel when you saw their beliefs? Did you feel committed to your own values?

After listening to other group members, would you like to modify your original list of values/beliefs? Why or why not? How did you deal with these newcomers? How did it feel to return to your group? Why?

Finish by linking the activity to the reality of cultural identity and the need to hold to personal values while being open to others. How did the feelings produced in this activity approximate those felt in other situations? How does this affect personal interaction? Racial and cultural tolerance? International tensions? How can we find ways of valuing differences rather than being bound by our own ways of seeing the world? What purposes are served by group and cultural identity?

THE MYSTERY CULTURE

Purpose

To place participants in a simulation which produces many of the features of an actual immersion in an unfamiliar culture. This activity should illustrate how much of communication is non-verbal, how our perception of different cultures is coloured by our own cultural values, and how it is dangerous to make judgements based on our bias.

Time Required: 2 to 3 hours.

Materials: Two rooms, one to be set up as the Albatrossian culture, and one where participants wait until they are taken to visit the Albatrossians; three large bowls, one for hand washing, one for food, and one for drink; sheets or other cloth to use for the dress of the Albatrossian man and woman; an unusual drink (could be of your own making, or some medicinal tea); unusual food, preferably of porridge-like consistency (may be coloured with bright food colouring); candles and incense for mood; a portable tape player, preferably with auto-reverse; and strange, soothing music (gamelan music from West Java is perfect, Japanese flute is good, or alternately, something New Age).

Notes on Use

The activity requires 4 or more facilitators, 3 to play the roles of the Albatrossians, and one to direct the participants into the 'scene.' It is best done with at least 12 participants, and works well with up to 20 or more. It is necessary to have a mixture of males and females.

The activity is very effective for simulating interactions

with foreign cultures. It functions on a number of levels, and if done with care, contains all the possible difficulties and dangers of real cross-cultural interaction.

A great deal of care should be taken to try to make the scene as foreign and strange as possible. Darkness, strange soothing music, candles, incense, and bizarre clothing all add to the atmosphere. It is important that no one particular culture is mimicked.

The ritual should be slow and drawn out. The Albatrossian whose duty it is to greet people when they arrive should be careful not to give too many cues to assist participants. Allow participants to discover for themselves who is to take their shoes off and who is to leave them on, who is to sit in the chairs and who must sit on the floor. The Albatrossians should let people know that they are acting inappropriately only through a mild hissing sound. The more difficulty that the participants experience, the better. This should be an emotional and experiential activity for participants, not just an academic exercise. Participants should experience the anxiety felt when encountering a very new and strange situation.

For the activity to work well, the facilitators must remain serious and inscrutable. Laughter and other disruptive activity should be immediately discouraged with mild hissing. Levity on the part of the facilitators is particularly damaging.

During the debriefing, it is important for the facilitators to focus on the participants' emotional responses as well as their intellectual interpretations.

Procedure

1. Facilitators should be well briefed as to the sequence of events in the script and to the described cultural values which underlie Albatrossian society. Prepare the Albatrossians' room in advance, keeping the participants in another area.

2. One facilitator should remain with the participants and

tell them that they are going to visit a mysterious people called Albatrossians, and that very little is known about these people except that they are hospitable, peaceful, and shy. Participants will have to use their powers of observation and their intuition during their visit. Since the Albatrossians are very shy, participants will be taken in small groups over a period of time.

3. The facilitator selects 2 participants to accompany him/her to the Albatrossians, asking the other participants to wait.

4. The facilitator and 2 participants go to the Albatrossians' room, at which point the activity unfolds according to the script.

5. Follow the simulation with a detailed and extensive debriefing.

Debriefing

The debriefing of this activity focusses on three areas. These are:

a. the feelings that the participants felt during the activity.

b. the skills that the participants employed to properly partake in the greeting ceremony.

c. the cultural assumptions that the participants made about the Albatrossians.

During the debriefing, emphasize that although this is an artificial situation, it closely parallels the emotions and mistakes that people make in actual cross-cultural experiences. The skills that the participants must employ to be effective during this activity are the same skills which are used in real cross-cultural situations.

1. Ask participants what their feelings were during the activity. Were they nervous, impatient, frustrated, angry, etc.?

Why? Was there any sort of sequence to the emotions? What effect did their feelings have on their behavior? Were the emotions a help or a hindrance in functioning in the Albatrossian society? How did the Albatrossians react to such behavior as inappropriate laughter, non-verbal expressions of anger, non-participation, etc.? How might people in real cross-cultural situations react to behavior such as inappropriate laughter during solemn ceremonies?

2. How did the participants figure out what to do during the ceremony? Have them make a list of the skills and techniques that they employed. Are these skills applicable in real life situations? Could the participants have been more effective in figuring out what to do? Was there anything that participants could do to be more effective? What things got in the way of the participants' effectiveness?

3. Ask the participants to identify the values of the Albatrossian culture. Allow them to elaborate upon these values as much as they see fit. Usually, participants identify the Albatrossian culture as one where women are subservient to men, along with other mistaken assumptions. These assumptions are the result of participants interpreting their observations based on their own cultural norms.

   When participants are finished identifying their assumptions, share with them the information on the cultural values of Albatrossian society. Invite their reactions, and ask for examples from their own lives where there were similar mistaken assumptions made about another culture.

   When confronting another culture, what are some valuable tactics to take to avoid mistaken assumptions? Is it valid to judge another culture based on your cultural norms? Discuss the statement 'Different cultural practices are not better or worse, only different.'

SCRIPT

The room with the Albatrossians should have the scene all set. An Albatrossian man and woman are the main hosts, and another Albatrossian (male or female) should greet guests at the door. Albatrossian men wear shoes and sit on chairs, Albatrossian women go barefoot and kneel on the floor next to the men. Good guests will be expected to do the same thing. The Albatrossian who greets the guests at the door will have the duty of escorting the participants to the circle of chairs. It will be this facilitator's responsibility to encourage the men to keep their shoes on and for the women to take their shoes off and leave them at the door. All communication by Albatrossians is in the special Albatrossian language. Albatrossians are a gentle, reserved, loving and sedate people who do not manhandle their guests. Touching is only done in ceremonial ways such as in their greetings. Thus, the effort to get the participants into their proper place and to remove or leave on their shoes is done principally through: (1) a gentle hiss, which indicates disapproval, (2) a hum, which indicates approval, and (3) a clicking of the tongue, which serves for all sorts of communication, such as getting-of-attention, transfer of information, etc. Although the Albatrossians are gentle and tolerant, they expect their guests to behave with decorum, and any laughing or talking among the guests will quickly receive a hiss from the Albatrossians.

The facilitator who is not playing the role of an Albatrossian should watch what happens to the first two participants. Once they are properly seated, with and without shoes, the facilitator should return to the main body of the participants and bring two or three more to the Albatrossians. This process should be repeated more quickly and with larger groups until all the participants are properly seated in a circle around the Albatrossian couple.

The next activity is the circle of greetings. The Albatrossian man gets up and greets each male participant around the circle in turn, by holding the participant by the shoulders and waist and rubbing their right legs together. After the greeting, the visitor should sit back down in the chair. Then the Albatrossian woman greets each female participant in turn around the circle. She kneels in front of a standing female guest and runs both hands down the lower legs and feet in a slow ceremonious way. After this greeting, the visitor should return to a sitting position.

After the greetings, a pause ensues during which all simply wait in silence. This pause should be prolonged for effect. During this and ensuing pauses, the Albatrossian man should, from time to time, gently push the woman's head towards the ground. The Albatrossians always maintain unsmiling (but serene and pleasant) expressions, and do not register in facial expressions their feelings and reactions to what may go on in the circle. Visitors who giggle or talk, or otherwise disturb the ritual are hissed at, but not with anger.

After the pause, a bowl of water is brought by the Albatrossian woman. Beginning with the Albatrossian man, each male in the circle dips the fingers of his right hand into the bowl and then waves them slowly and gracefully in the air to dry them. After all the males in the circle have washed their hands, the Albatrossian woman returns to her place by the Albatrossian man and another pause ensues. The women in the circle do not wash their hands.

At a clicking cue from the Albatrossian man, the Albatrossian woman rises and offers food to each male in turn, beginning with the Albatrossian man. She sticks her hands into the food, and stuffs a little of it into the man's mouth. Upon being fed, the Albatrossian man indicates his appreciation by a loud hum which is accompanied by a rubbing of the stomach. After the men are fed, the Albatrossian woman then feeds each of the women in turn, finally ending with herself. After the meal is finished, the Albatrossian woman again returns to her place and there is another pause in the ritual.

The next step is the serving of drink. In the same manner as with the food, the Albatrossian woman serves the Albatrossian male, and then all the other males, a drink. She then serves all the women guests before returning to her place kneeling beside the Albatrossian man. Again there is a pause during which the Albatrossian man gently pushes the Albatrossian woman's head to the ground.

After a clicking cue from the Albatrossian man, the Albatrossians rise and proceed around the circle of guests communicating with one another with clicking sounds. Without making clear indications to the participants , they choose the woman guest with the largest feet, who is led over to the Albatrossian man's chair. She, like the Albatrossian woman, kneels beside the Albatrossian man, who again gently pushes both the women's heads to the floor.

The last activity of the ceremony is a repeat of the greeting. The Albatrossian man rises and makes a circuit of the guests, greeting each of the male participants. The Albatrossian woman follows, greeting each of the female participants. The two Albatrossians then indicate to the selected participant who is still kneeling by the chair to follow them, and the three people leave the circle, which concludes this part of the activity.

CULTURAL VALUES OF
ALBATROSSIAN SOCIETY

Since part of the purpose of this activity is to show the danger of making cultural assumptions about other societies based on the values framework of one's own society, it is important that all the facilitators share a unified and consistent understanding of Albatrossian society.

Although participants usually assume otherwise, the Albatrossians value women above men. The earth is sacred and all fruitfulness is blessed. Consequently, women, who bring life into being, are sacred and because of their sacred status, only they are permitted to be in direct contact with the earth. They alone may go barefoot and sit directly upon the ground. Their greeting emphasizes the earth and women's connection with it. Only women are allowed to prepare and serve the fruits of the earth.

The roles of men and women in Albatrossian society reflect their differing relationships to the earth. The Albatrossian man pushes the kneeling woman's head towards the ground as part of his duty to remind the woman of her sacred connection with the earth. He eats and drinks first to protect her and all that she represents from harm and defilement.

The society of the Albatrossians values serenity and calm. They put great store in the stateliness and ceremony of their rituals, and expect others to value these things. They are peaceful and welcoming of strangers, and they expect their guests to enter into their rituals with proper respect and decorum. They, like most other cultures, assume that the way they do things and view the world are natural, rational, and universal to all humans. Consequently, they assume that the guests would want to be welcomed ritually and would understand that the woman with the largest feet should receive special honours because she has the greatest direct contact with the earth as she walks upon it.

CAUSES OF RACISM

Purpose

To provide participants with an opportunity to look at the causes behind racism and prejudice and to strategize solutions.

Time Required: 1 to $1\frac{1}{2}$ hours.

Materials: Research on the Causes of Racism sheets for each participant, master list of causes of racism on flip chart paper (with space for volunteered causes), three blank flip chart sheets and markers, adhesive-backed coloured dots, pen and paper for each group of 4 or 5.

Notes on Use

Prejudice and racism do not come from nowhere. Studies show that young children are generally oblivious to racial differences until they are about 4 or 5. Negative attitudes do not appear until they are introduced through the school, home, and media, and through peers and adults. Many students may not have thought about the roots of racism, and this exercise is designed to have them reflect both on the causes of prejudice and racism and some possible solutions. Racism is a learned attitude; it can be unlearned.

The list of causes presented here is a loose collection of experiences and messages based on research that has been done on the causes of racism. It is not intended to be exhaustive, but because many students may not have thought much about this issue, the list is designed to provide them with some concepts to reflect on; it should stimulate further thinking and ideas around this issue. The dots are used to actively involve participants in expressing their opinion on the most important causes of racism; the 5 top choices can be used as the basis for strategizing solutions.

You may wish to rewrite the list of causes in simpler language to accommodate the group you are working with. As well, you can combine some causes to make the list less difficult if you are working with younger students or those with lower reading skills. Be sure that the participants fully understand each cause.

If you do not have the time to write the causes out on the chart paper, copy the list of causes and cut it into strips, each strip containing one cause. Then tape these onto a piece of flip chart paper. Allow enough space at the bottom to write in additional causes. Whether you tape the causes onto the paper or write them out, make sure the master list of the causes of racism to be posted on the wall provides a wide enough margin to the left of the factors listed to accommodate dots.

Procedure

1. Explain to students that racism is a learned attitude that has definite roots. The activity they are going to participate in will help them to look at some of the factors that contribute to racist attitudes.

2. Place students in groups of 4 or 5 and distribute the Research on the Causes of Racism sheet. Answer questions they may have about the ideas presented or the vocabulary used and, most importantly, discuss each factor in terms of their own experience. Take a few minutes to circulate among the groups to make sure they understand the ideas.

3. Explain to the participants that this is an incomplete list of some of the possible causes of racism. Have them brainstorm any additional causes they can think of based

on their experience and awareness. Instruct them to add these to the list.

4. Assuming the items on the Racism sheet have been transferred to pieces of flip chart paper, add any new ideas brainstormed in the groups, combining similar ideas as required. Post this master list on a wall.

5. Hand out 3 self-adhesive dots to each participant. Explain that the particpants are to study the causes of racism identified and decide which are the main contributors to the development of racist attitudes. Then have them place a dot by each of the 3 items they feel is most critical.

6. Once the dots have been placed, review the master list. Which items have received the most dots? Place the 3 items with the most dots on separate sheets of chart paper and post on the wall. In their groups, have students strategize ideas for overcoming each of these 3 causes of racism. Have a recorder for each group write the ideas on paper, one piece of paper for each cause.

7. As a large group, combine the strategies onto the flip chart paper for each cause. Discuss these in terms of how they could be implemented and whether they would result in a reduction of racist attitudes.

Debriefing

Have students reflect on the activity: How did you arrive at your personal choice of the top three factors? What personal influences and experiences affected your decision? What did you learn about the causes of racism? About the solutions? How practical were the solutions suggested?

Why does racism persist? Whose interests does it serve? What can *we* do to counteract racism?

RESEARCH ON THE CAUSES OF RACISM

1. Disapproval in the media or from adults of attempts by members of minority groups to attain equality and greater power for themselves.

2. Absence of minority people as positive role models.

3. Emphasis on problems experienced by ethnic groups without information on the underlying socio/historical causes of the problems.

4. Information and activities that stress differences between cultural and ethnic groups rather than similarities.

5. As children, observing negative responses of parents and other adults to people from minority cultures and ethnic groups (avoidance, disapproval, condemnation, slurs).

6. Continuing lower position of visible minorities in society leads to the conclusion that minority groups are less well-liked, are inferior, and deserve to be treated unequally.

7. Condescending or stereotypical portrayal of minority groups in television programs, films, cartoons, newspapers, magazines, and other media.

8. Absence of minority persons in high-profile and powerful positions in Canadian society.

9. Lack of knowledge about culture and cultural differences.

10. Education that fails to teach multiculturalism, racial tolerance, and cultural understanding.

11. School materials that present stereotypical views of minority cultural groups.

12. Omission in schools and in home of information on the

role played by minority cultures in Canadian history and in contemporary society.

13. Insufficient positive contact with members of minority cultural groups.

14. The need for visible and vulnerable scapegoats to blame for social, economic, and personal difficulties.

15. Misconceptions about immigrants and their impact on Canadian society.

FACES: AN EXERCISE
IN PRECONCEPTIONS

Purpose

To demonstrate the preconceptions and judgements which are often made based on race, gender, or appearance.

Time Required: 30 to 45 minutes.

Materials: Approximately 8 pictures of people of different ages, genders, and races.

Notes on Use

This exercise can be used with First Nations groups, multicultural groups and/or mainstream Canadian groups with equal effect. Obviously, the participants have no real basis for choosing individuals which fit the descriptions of step 2, but the facilitator should encourage them to answer each of the questions and examine why they made those choices later in step 3.

Procedure

1. Number each picture, pass it around the group, and then post it at the front of the room where everyone can see it.

2. Instruct participants to write down their answers to the following questions about the pictures:

    a. If you needed help in a strange town, which one of the individuals would you approach for assistance?

b. Which of the individuals would you not want to ask for help?

c. Which of the individuals do you think is most successful?

d. Which of the individuals would you like as a friend?

e. Which of the individuals do you think is most intelligent?

f. Which of the individuals is the most caring parent?

g. Which of the individuals is most likely on social assistance?

h. Which of the individuals is a recent immigrant to Canada?

i. Which of the individuals is illiterate?

j. Which of the individuals is an alcoholic?

3. When participants are finished, have them form triads and share their answers with one another, attempting to explain why they made the choices they did. The facilitator should circulate amongst the triads and listen to the discussions.

4. Form the large group again and tabulate the results of which picture was chosen for each of the questions in step two.

Identify any trends which become apparent and discuss some of the biases and stereotypes that have emerged.

Debriefing

The purpose of the activity is to attempt to illustrate that everyone has a natural tendency to make judgements and assumptions. These preconceptions and stereotypes can be both negative and positive (e.g., the "noble savage"), but both types stand in the way of genuine cross-cultural interaction and communication.

What were some of the preconceptions and stereotypes which came out? Was any particular race or gender viewed more negatively than another?

Were people more apt to be positive about or to feel drawn to their own race or gender? Why?

Was the person most chosen as a recent immigrant a visible minority? Why was this?

What did participants learn from this activity?

FACES: An exercise in preconceptions

questions	picture 1	picture 2	picture 3	picture 4	picture 5	picture 6	picture 7	picture 8
a								
b								
c								
d								
e								
f								
g								

WORLD MAPPING

Purpose

To explore participants' knowledge about the physical and political geography of the world.

Time Required: $1\frac{1}{2}$ to 2 hours.

Materials: World and/or continental maps; atlases; assorted markers and crayons; 6 sheets of newsprint of the following sizes:

#1 medium sheet (1 m. x $1\frac{1}{2}$ m.) (North America)

#2 medium sheet (1 m. x 1 $\frac{1}{2}$ m .) (South America)

#3 small sheet ($\frac{3}{4}$ m. x $\frac{3}{4}$ m.) (Europe)

#4 large sheet $1\frac{1}{3}$ m. x $1\frac{1}{3}$ m.) (Africa)

#5 very large sheet (2 m. x $1\frac{3}{4}$ m.) (Asia)

#6 L-shaped sheet (long leg large) (Australasia and the Pacific)

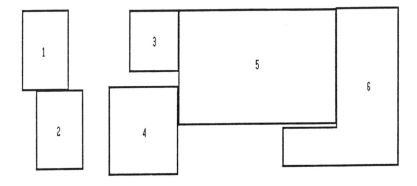

Notes on Use

This activity is designed to examine some of the implications of ethnocentricity of the mainstream culture. The facilitator may want to emphasize that knowledge or ignorance of regions of the world are a direct result of the media and the educational system rather than a personal failing. The activity works well with both homogeneous and heterogeneous groups.

Procedure:

1. Instruct participants to form 6 groups.

2. Assign each group a continent and instruct them to draw as detailed a map as possible of:

   —North America, Central America, and the Caribbean.

   —South America.

   —Europe, to the Ural Mountains.

   —Africa.

   —Asia, including Asia Minor, the Middle East, the Indian sub-continent, and S.E. Asia excluding the Indonesian Archipelago.

   —The Indonesian Archipelago, Australasia and the Pacific Islands.

The maps should be drawn without the aid of other maps or atlases, and should include:

   —Political boundaries—national, state/provincial.

   —Current names of countries.

   —Capital cities and other major cities.

   —Major geographical features—lakes, rivers, seas, bays, mountain ranges, deserts, etc.

   —Major exports and resources.

—Brief written descriptions of any significant political or current events in the regions

3. Allow 45 minutes for the groups to attempt to complete their task. During this initial attempt, the groups should be working entirely independently.

4. After 45 minutes, allow participants to freely circulate and help make corrections and additions to other groups' maps.

5. Tape all of the maps together on the floor to make a large world map.

6. Provide maps and atlases to participants and allow them time to analyse how well they did.

Debriefing

Ask participants how they felt about their ability to accurately portray their assigned region politically and physically. Did they do better or worse than they might have expected?

Ask participants to identify which regions were easiest for them, and which were most difficult. Why is this so? It is expected that North America should be familiar to participants, but why are other regions also familiar? Why are other regions unfamiliar?

Often Europe is more familiar to Canadian groups than Africa or Asia. Why might this be? Did more participants know where Japan is situated than where Bhutan is? Why would one geographically small Asian country be better known than another?

What are the reasons that we are familiar with some regions or countries and not others? Is it the result of recent newsworthy events, of economic prominence, or of a cultural bias in the Canadian education system?

What are some of the implications of familiarity or ignorance of other regions of the world as far as government decisions about foreign policy or immigration? What are the implications of this gap of knowledge for public perceptions of international issues?

WORLD WEB

Purpose

To visually portray global interdependence as it relates to group members.

Time Required: 30 to 45 minutes.

Materials: The large maps created during the World Mapping activity, or a chalk outline world map drawn on the floor, or sheets of flip chart paper, and a ball of yarn or twine.

Notes on Use

Ideally, this activity is a follow-up to the World Mapping activity. It is convenient to make use of the world map created in that activity; however, with a bit of ingenuity, the activity can stand alone. If World Mapping has not been done, a very basic chalk outline of the world can be drawn on the floor. If that is not possible, use sheets of flip chart paper which can be labelled to represent continents and placed on the floor in the correct relative positions. It is important to remember that the representations of the various areas of the world must be large enough to allow groups of people to stand upon them. Since travel between the U.S. and Canada is so common, the U.S. will not be considered as foreign in the questions asked below.

Procedure

1. Stand on the map on the spot that as closely as possible approximates the actual location of the group.

2. Ask all participants who were born in another country (excluding the U.S.) to stand on that country on the map.

When they are in place, throw the ball of yarn to one person, and instruct her or him to hold onto the yarn and throw the ball back. Throw it to another person, and continue on this way so that a web of yarn begins to develop with you as the 'hub' and with 'spokes' of yarn connecting each participant with the 'hub.'

3. Now ask any of the remaining participants who have lived in another country (excluding the U.S.) to go to that country. Repeat the process with the yarn.

4. Ask questions until everyone is on another country and connected to you by the yarn. Remember to exclude the U.S. as foreign. Questions might include anyone who:

—has a parent or spouse who was born in another country.

—has grandparents born in another country.

—has travelled to another country.

—drives a car from another country.

—is wearing clothes from another country.

—has eaten food that day which originated in another country (sugar, coffee, tea, bananas, chocolate, etc.).

5. Ask participants to reflect on the web that they are enmeshed in. Instruct them to disentangle themselves.

Debriefing

Ask participants what they thought of the web formed by the activity. What has this activity to do with global interdependence? Did the activity make the linkages that we all have with other areas of the world any more concrete?

Ask participants to comment on whether they were surprised at the personal connections that exist within the group. Assist the participants to realize what a rich source of knowledge, viewpoints, and information those personal connections can provide the group.

VIEWS OF MAN
AND NATURE

Purpose

To examine First Nations' and Western views of the world and man's relationship to it.

Time Required: 1 hour.

Materials: A copy of Chief Seattle's speech and Genesis 1:1-28 for each participant. **Note:** New discoveries have shown that Chief Seattle's speech is actually a fairly recently written piece based on an earlier account of Chief Seattle's oral reply to Washington. The speech is still used because it is representative of a view of the world shared in the traditional stories of most First Nations people.

Notes on Use

Some people may be offended by using the passage from Genesis in an examination of the foundations of European values and world views. Other cultures have creation 'stories' or 'myths,' while one's own cultural traditions are the 'truth.' This in itself might become an interesting topic of discussion arising out of this activity.

The First Nations had many different traditional stories, but a common element in the stories of all First Nations people is the concept of brotherhood with the other species which inhabit the earth. Raven or Coyote are not fundamentally different creatures from humans; they change skins to assume human or animal form.

Procedure

1. Introduce the activity with a short talk about cultural values. Values are the non-material aspects of a culture. They are a learned body of knowledge which influence how we perceive the world around us and what we consider to be normal acceptable behaviour in that world. Values are shaped in a large part by the traditional stories (some call them myths) which are passed down within the cultural system.

2. Ask participants to identify the traditional stories which were important to the Europeans who arrived to settle Canada. There can be a number of answers here—Greek and Roman myths, folk and fairy tales—but above all else, the most important stories which instilled the values of the Europeans were the stories from the Bible.

3. Hand out copies of Genesis 1:1 - 28 and read aloud as a group. Have participants form into small groups and list the values and the views of the world that this passage expresses and teaches. When participants have finished, reform a large group and have them share their results with one another. Keep a master record of these on flip chart paper which is laid out as follows:

GENESIS / WESTERN	CHIEF SEATTLE / FIRST NATIONS

4. Pass out copies of Chief Seattle's speech. Explain who Chief Seattle was and where and when he lived, and that this is actually a revised version of Chief Seattle's oral reply to a query that the U.S. government made in 1852 about buying tribal lands for settlers. Read the passage for participants. When you have finished, ask them to read it through again on their own, and in their small groups, write down the main points that reflect the traditional world view and values of First Nations people.

5. Have participants reform as a large group and share with one another the views and values they have identified. Record these results on the master chart.

6. Examine the similarities and differences of the two views of the world as represented on the master chart. Contrast the values and the attitudes contained in the 2 documents. Ask participants to identify some of the results that have come about because of these two radically different ways of seeing the world and man's place in it.

Debriefing

The Genesis passage expresses some of the core differences that exist between the world views of the European settlers of Canada and the First Nations inhabitants of Canada. Only humans were created in God's image, the plants and animals, even the earth itself, was put under man's dominion. Mankind was commanded by God to multiply their kind and to subdue the earth.

How do the values and teachings of the Genesis passage fit with the traditional Western model of resource use and management?

How does this compare with the lessons of the First Nations traditional stories and the values that they imbued in the members of those cultures? Did the U.S. government pay any attention to Chief Seattle's conditions for selling the land?

Chief Seattle says, "How can you buy or sell the sky? The land? The idea is strange to us." Are there any similar ideas about ownership of resources in the western tradition? Can individuals own land below the high water mark on lakes, rivers or oceans? Can someone own the water in the lakes and rivers? (Yes, in some circumstances, e.g., irrigation rights.) What would happen if someone claimed to own the air and demanded payment from people? Why do you think that Europeans developed this concept of individual land owner-ship?

Chief Seattle's view of the world and his relationship with it are becoming popular again in Canada, not only with First Nations people, but with non-Natives as well. It is a concept called stewardship. What do you think stewardship involves?

GENESIS 1:1-28

1. In the beginning God created the heaven and the earth.

2. And the earth was without form, and void; and darkness [was] upon the face of the deep. And the Spirit of God moved upon the face of the waters.

3. And God said, Let there be light: and there was light.

4. And God saw the light, that [it was] good: and God divided the light from the darkness.

5. And God called the light Day, and the darkness he called Night. And the evening and the morning were the first day.

6. And God said, Let there be a firmament in the midst of the waters, and let it divide the waters from the waters.

7. And God made the firmament, and divided the waters which [were] under the firmament from the waters which [were] above the firmament: and it was so.

8. And God called the firmament Heaven. And the evening and the morning were the second day.

9. And God said, Let the waters under the heaven be gathered together unto one place, and let the dry [land] appear: and it was so.

10. And God called the dry [land] Earth; and the gathering together of the waters called the Seas: and God saw that [it was] good.

11. And God said, Let the earth bring forth grass, the herb yielding seed, [and] the fruit tree yielding fruit after his kind, whose seed [is] in itself, upon the earth: and it was so.

12. And the earth brought forth grass, [and] herb yielding seed after his kind, and the tree yielding fruit, whose seed

[was] in itself, after his kind: and God saw that [it was] good.

13. And the evening and the morning were the third day.

14. And God said, Let there be lights in the firmament of the heaven to divide the day from the night; and let them be for signs, and for seasons, and for days, and years:

15. And let them be for lights in the firmament of the heaven to give light upon the earth: and it was so.

16. And God made two great lights; the greater light to rule the day, and the lesser light to rule the night: [he made] the stars also.

17. And God set them in the firmament of the heaven to give light upon the earth,

18. And to rule over the day and over the night, and to divide the light from the darkness: and God saw that [it was] good.

19. And the evening and the morning were the fourth day.

20. And God said, Let the waters bring forth abundantly the moving creature that hath life, and fowl [that] may fly above the earth in the open firmament of heaven.

21. And God created great whales, and every living creature that moveth, which the waters brought forth abundantly, after their kind, and every winged fowl after his kind: and God saw that [it was] good.

22. And God blessed them, saying, Be fruitful, and multiply, and fill the waters in the seas, and let fowl multiply in the earth.

23. And the evening and the morning were the fifth day.

24. And God said, Let the earth bring forth the living creature after his kind, cattle, and creeping thing, and beast of the earth after his kind: and it was so.

25. And God made the beast of the earth after his kind, and cattle after their kind, and every thing that creepeth upon the earth after his kind: and God saw that [it was] good.

26. And God said, Let us make man in our image, after our likeness: and let them have dominion over the fish of the sea, and over the fowl of the air, and over the cattle, and over all the earth, and over every creeping thing that creepeth upon the earth.

27. So God created man in his [own] image, in the image of God created he him; male and female created he them.

28. And God blessed them, and God said unto them, Be fruitful, and multiply, and replenish the earth, and subdue it: and have dominion over the fish of the sea, and over the fowl of the air, and over every living thing that moveth upon the earth.

CHIEF SEATTLE'S SPEECH

"The President in Washington sends word that he wishes to buy our land. But how can you buy or sell the sky? The land? The idea is strange to us. If we do not own the freshness of the air and sparkle of the water, how can you buy them?

"Every part of this earth is sacred to my people. Every shining pine needle, every sandy shore, every mist in the dark woods, every meadow, every humming insect. All holy in the memory and experience of my people.

"We know the sap which courses through the trees as we know the blood that courses through our veins. We are part of the earth and it is part of us. The perfumed flowers are our sisters. The bear, the deer, the great eagle, these are our brothers. The rocky crests, the juices in the meadow, the body heat of the pony, and man, all belong to the same family.

"The shining water that moves in the streams and rivers is not just water, but the blood of our ancestors. If we sell you our land, you must remember that it is sacred. Each ghostly reflection in the clear waters of the lakes tells of events and memories in the life of my people. The water's murmur is the voice of my father's father.

"The rivers are our brothers. They quench our thirst. They carry our canoes and feed our children. So you must give to the rivers the kindness you would give any brother.

"If we sell you our land, remember that the air is precious to us, that the air shares its spirit with all the life it supports. The wind that gave our grandfather his first breath also receives his last sigh. The wind also gives our children the spirit of life. So if we sell you our land, you must keep it apart and sacred, as a place where man can go to taste the wind that is sweetened by the meadow flowers.

"Will you teach your children what we have taught our children? That the earth is our mother? What befalls the earth befalls all the sons of the earth.

"This we know: the earth does not belong to man, man

belongs to the earth. All things are connected like the blood that unites us all. Man did not weave the web of life, he is merely a strand in it. Whatever he does to the web, he does to himself.

"One thing we know: our god is also your god. The earth is precious to him and to harm the earth is to heap contempt on his creator.

"Your destiny is a mystery to us. What will happen when the buffalo are all slaughtered? The wild horses tamed? What will happen when the secret corners of the forest are heavy with the scent of many men and the view of the ripe hills is blotted by talking wires? Where will the thicket be? Gone! Where will the eagle be? Gone! And what is it to say goodbye to the swift pony and the hunt? The end of living and the beginning of survival.

"When the last Red Man has vanished with his wilderness and his memory is only the shadow of a cloud moving across the prairie, will these shores and forests still be here? Will there be any of the spirit of my people left?

"We love this earth as a newborn loves its mother's heartbeat. So, if we sell you our land, love it as we have loved it. Care for it as we have cared for it. Hold in your mind the memory of the land as it is when you receive it. Preserve the land for all children and love it, as God loves us all.

"As we are part of the land, you too are part of the land. This earth is precious to us. It is also precious to you. One thing we know: there is only one God. No man, be he Red Man or White Man, can be apart. We are brothers, after all."

Chief Seattle's reply, in 1852, to the U.S. government's inquiry about buying tribal lands for the arriving settlers. Reprinted in The Power of Myth *by Joseph Campbell with Bill Moyers (Doubleday, 1988).*

FAMILIES

Purpose

To examine traditional family structure and to determine to what extent traditional family structure exists in contemporary societies.

Time Required: 1½ hours.

Materials: assorted coloured marking pens and flip chart paper for each participant.

Notes on Use

Although this activity is not meant to be therapeutic, it may be difficult or stressful for participants who have unhappy or negative associations with the concept of family. Be aware of individual reactions to the activity, and spend as much time as necessary debriefing the emotions which may emerge.

Procedure

1. Hand out pens and paper and have participants draw a picture of their family. Try not to give too much direction, which may unduly influence the product. Instruct them to include everyone they feel is their family, regardless of the western notion that a family consists of mom, dad, and the kids. If a biological father was not part of their life, then the father would have no place in the picture; conversely, if cousins, aunts, uncles, etc., played an important part in their everyday lives, then they should be included in the picture. When everyone is finished,

have them break into groups of 3 and share their pictures with one another.

2. When participants have finished the sharing, ask how many of them had western-style nuclear families. How many were just mother and children? How many had a more extended family in which uncles, aunts, cousins and other relations were considered important family members? Explain that households such as these are called extended families and that this is the common type of family structure for many societies in the world. Do participants know what type of family structure was common in traditional First Nations society? (Answer: the extended family.)

3. Have participants take their pictures and use them as the basis for creating a simple family tree. Any participants who are related to one another may work together on this. These family trees should include all the people identified as family members in the pictures, and as many others as the participant can identify. Participants should then be asked to try and work back as many generations as possible, through great-grandparents, great-great-grandparents, etc. How far back can they go? Do they have any sense of when these ancestors were born and when they lived? If participants are native, which bands did these ancestors belong to and where did they live? What did they do for a living? Instruct participants to form dyads and share their family trees with each other.

4. (Optional activity) Refer to the passage on pages 36-41 in My Heart Soars by Chief Dan George. Clarify with participants who Chief Dan George was. This passage deals with Chief Dan George's recollections of a more traditional, extended family structure. Read the passage to the participants, paying special attention to any points which Chief Dan George makes about the idea of family.

a) Have participants identify the points which the article

makes about the family. What are some of the implications of the Squamish traditional view of family?

b) How does the traditional Squamish view of the family as detailed by Chief Dan George compare with the traditional view of the family as seen by participants' cultural groups?

c) How does it compare with the contemporary view of the family as seen by participants' cultural groups?

d) How does the traditional Squamish view of the family compare with the typically 'Canadian' contemporary view of the family?

e) Relate the points made about the family in the article with the pictures that participants have drawn.

f) Do the participants agree with Chief Dan George's statement that "Soon it will be too late to know my culture, for integration is upon us and soon we will have no values but yours"? Why or why not?

GENDER AND WORK

Purpose

To examine the changing roles and labour of men and women in First Nations culture.

Time Required: 1 to 1½ hours.

Materials: Flip chart paper and markers.

Notes on Use

The purpose of this activity is to examine the changes in First Nations cultures shown by the changing roles of men and women. In the first step of the procedure, it is important that participants focus on traditional First Nations societies in general. Step 2 requires that they personalize their examination of the issue and try to get a sense of the changes in their societies by examining their own family history.

If participants have done the activity 'First Nations Families,' they may want to refer to the pictures and the family trees that they created to assist them in this activity.

Procedure

1. Post two sheets of flip chart paper. Write MEN at the top of one and WOMEN at the top of the other. Have participants brainstorm the work which women were responsible for in traditional First Nations culture and the work which men did, and record the results on the flip chart paper.

WORK IN TRADITIONAL SOCIETIES

MEN'S	WOMEN'S

2. Instruct participants to study the results and observe whether any generalizations can be made about the kinds of labour that women and men did in traditional First Nations society (i.e.: interesting, physical, at home, away from home). What was the relative economic importance of men's and women's labour in traditional society? Do participants think that men and women worked approximately the same number of hours, or did one sex work more than the other?

3. Have participants record on a flip chart the work that the women in each of their families did over as long a time span as they can accurately remember (i.e.: daughters, sisters, mothers, aunts, grandmothers, great-grandmothers). This work should not be confined to the paid labour which is now currently thought of as work; it should also include work which is not part of the wage system, such as traditional food gathering and processing.

4. Have them do the same for the men in their families.

5. Instruct participants to form triads and share their results. One member of the group should keep notes and present a summary of their discussions of the following

points: Do you notice any trends over time? Whose work changed the most, men's or women's? Has either group had their workload increased or decreased? Has there been a blending or merging of the labour roles of First Nations men and women? Considering all work done, paid and unpaid, who spends the greater number of hours working, men or women?

6. Bring the group together and have representatives from each of the triads share some of the results of their discussions and try to identify patterns of change in men's and women's labour in First Nations societies.

Debriefing

Who is more likely to be paid for their labour? As far as power and decision-making in the family are concerned, what are the implications of being paid for work?

What have been the implications for the equality of men and women in adopting a western-style wage economy? Did women have more or less power in traditional First Nations society? Why or why not?

What is the representation of men and women in the group? Is there equal representation of men and women? Why might this be?

Should half of all seats in the training programs be reserved for women?

CHARACTERISTICS OF A NATIVE COMMUNITY

Purpose

To review the recollections of a Native elder about the community in which he grew up, and to attempt to identify characteristics common to many Native communities.

Time Required: 1½ to 2 hours.

Materials: "Childhood in an Indian Village" (abridged) by Wilfred Pelletier, an Ontario Native elder; "Characteristics of a Native Community" discussion paper; flip chart or blackboard; felt pens or chalk.

Notes on Use

This article was written a number of years ago, but reflects the values and beliefs many Native people grew up with, particularly children in more remote and isolated communities. It provides a basis for reflecting on traditional Native community characteristics, their modern-day relevance, and ways to strengthen them. Because of the length of the article, you may wish to pass it out the day before the activity to allow students time to read it in preparation for the activity phase.

Procedure

1. Hand out the Pelletier article to the students and ask them to read it. As they are reading or after they have finished, ask them to list the values, beliefs, world view

concepts, and community characteristics they find in the text.

2. When the students have finished reading and have listed their characteristics, divide the class into groups of 3 and hand out the "Characteristics of a Native Community" discussion paper.

3. Instruct groups to go through the questions one by one and discuss them, recording students' positions on each one. Discussion should focus on trying to find a common position on the issues, but the variety of ideas and positions presented should also be noted.

4. Once the groups have finished the discussion paper, have them appoint a spokesperson to read aloud the group's responses to the questions, allowing for input from the rest of the students.

5. On a flip chart or blackboard, record the highlights of each group's responses. Help to identify similarities and differences in responses.

6. Consolidate similar comments so that common points are established for debriefing.

Debriefing

Debriefing can take a number of directions depending on the kind of students you are working with and your purposes. A group of educators might identify how the concept of community reflected in the article could inform a band education program or translate into teaching materials. Community developers might discuss how the strengths could be built upon toward a holistic community development. School-age students could simply examine the community profile as a way of identifying and discussing traditional community values and organization, comparing them to modern-day situations.

What kind of values, behaviours and attitudes have been

retained in Pelletier's home community? Which have been lost? Why?

How would having this kind of background be helpful to a teacher, community health worker, or community development consultant? How important is it for people working in communities to have an overview of the community's history and mores?

How does Pelletier's community compare to the one in which you grew up? What are the similarities and differences? What are the strengths and weaknesses of Pelletier's community? How can the strengths be built upon?

How can traditional values play a role in contemporary society and in community development?

CHILDHOOD IN AN INDIAN VILLAGE
by Wilfred Pelletier

Going back as far as I can remember as a child in an Indian community, I had no sense of knowing about the other people around me except that we were all somehow equal; the class structure in the community was horizontal. There was only one class. Nobody was interested in getting on top of anybody else.

You could see it in our games. Nobody organized them. There weren't any competitive sports. But we were involved in lots of activity (I was not like I am now; I was in pretty good shape at that time) and we were organized, but not in the sense that there were ways of finding out who had won and who had lost. We played ball like everyone else, but no one kept score. In fact, you would stay up at bat until you hit the ball. If somebody happened to walk by on the street, an old guy, we'd tease him and bug him to come over and try to hit the ball, and he would come over and he'd swing away. If they threw us out on first, we'd stay on first anyway. We ran to second, and they would throw us out there, and sometimes we'd get thrown out all the way around.

It was later on in life that I began to realize that what we were really doing was playing. Very much like animals play. When you observe the bear, the adult, the male and female are always playing with the cubs. The otters do the same thing. None of the kind of play we had was really structured and organized. That came after the recreation directors from the outside world came in and told us that we had a problem in the community, that we were not organized, and they were going to introduce some.

They introduced it all right, and the tremendous competitiveness that went with it. It's not bad on Manitoulin Island, where I'm from, as it is in a lot of places where competitiveness is rolling in. I'm glad I can remember that as a kid I was able to become involved with a community with others and nobody was competing. Even if we did formally compete in the games we did, no one was a winner though someone may have won. It was only the moment. If you beat someone by pulling a bow and arrow and shooting the arrow further, it only meant that you shot the arrow farther at that moment. That's all it lasted. It didn't mean you were better in any way whatsoever. It just meant that at that particular time the arrow went further; maybe it was just the way you let the bow go.

One of the very important things was the relationship we had with our families. We didn't always live at home. We lived wherever we happened to be at that particular time when it got dark. If you were two or three miles away from home, then that is where you slept. People would feed you even if they didn't know who you were. We'd spend an evening, perhaps, with an old couple, and they would tell us stories. Most of these stories were legends, and they were told to us mostly in the wintertime. In the summer, people would generally take us out and we would do a number of things which in some way would allow us to learn about life and what it was all about: that is, by talking about some particular person and demonstrating what that person did. At no time, in all the years I spent there, do I ever remember anyone teaching us anything.

I have been to numerous communities across Canada and I still do not find where Indians teach. All young children were allowed to grow, to develop, to learn. They didn't teach you that this was mommy, daddy, desk, ashtray, house, etc. We learned about these things by listening to the words adults spoke, what they said when they were talking, and built our own kind of relationship with the article. If you observe your children now you will see a child turn a chair over, cover it with a blanket and use it for a house. He can relate many ways to a chair. As we get older we have only one relationship and that is to stick our rear ends on that chair. It's for no other purpose and, in fact, we tell our kids that that is what it is, and it belongs in a corner and don't move it out of there.

These things I remember very well. We were brought up to have a different relationship to a house and to all the things that surrounded us. That is, the values that adults placed on things in the community did not necessarily carry over into their child and lead him to place the same values on them. Children discovered the values of these things on their own, and developed their own particular relationship to them. This is how they learned.

It was a very different kind of learning situation that we were in as children. In fact, all of the things we did related to our way of life. Everything had to fit into the whole; we didn't learn things in parts. As an example: if we watched someone running an outboard motor, we would learn everything that was involved in working with that motor. If someone taught someone here to do that, after he was finished he might add a safety program on top of it. This would be an additional thing. The way Indians learned it, they built in a safety program while they were learning through their observations and because their lives depended on their doing it right.

And just as we didn't separate our learning from our way of life, we didn't separate our work from it either. The older women, for example, who used to work all day at whatever— tanning hides, etc.—didn't really think of it as work. It was a way of life. That's the real difference between the kind of society we have now where we equate these kinds of things with work and yet will go out and play sports and enjoy it and the kind of society I'm talking about. Here we go and work and use maybe half or a quarter of the energy we spend playing sports, but we call it work and we feel differently about it altogether. These are the kinds of differences that exist. Indian people who had a way of life and who felt it was their way of life didn't call it work. It was a part of the way they provided for their families; and they "worked" very hard.

One of the reasons, of course, why they didn't call it "work" was that they didn't have any foremen. As I mentioned before, there wasn't any kind of a vertical structure in the community. In these communities what existed was a sharing of power. In spite of what everybody says, we really didn't have chiefs, that is, people who were bosses. We had medicine men who were wise men. The rest were leaders in particular ways. They weren't leaders as we look at them today. It was a different kind of leadership in that the person who was leader had then discarded the leadership when he was finished with the job. He had power only for the time he wanted to do something. That power came in all forms of all the things he did in the community, so that he used power only for the things he wanted to do, and then he immediately shed it so that someone else could pick it up and it could change hands several times in the community in a day or a week or whatever.

Our language is so important to us as a people. Our language and our language structure related to our whole way of life. How beautiful that picture language is where they only tell you the beginning and the end, and you fill in everything, and they allow you to feel how you want to feel. Here we manipulate and twist things around and get you to hate a guy. The Indian doesn't do that. He'll just say that some guy got into an accident, and he won't give you any details. From then on you just explore as far as you want to. You'll say, "What happened?" and he'll tell you a little more. "Did he go through the windshield?" "Yep!" He only answers questions. All of the in-between you fill in for yourself as you see it. We are losing that feeling when we lose our language at school. We are taught English, not Indian, as our first language. And that changes our relationship with our parents. All of a sudden we begin saying to our parents, "You're stupid." We have begun to equate literacy with learning, and this is the first step down. It is we who are going down and not our parents, and because of that separation we are going down lower on the rung because it is we who are rejecting our parents; they are not rejecting us. The parents know that, but they are unable to do anything about it. And we take on the values and the history of somebody else.

Maybe storytelling happens among other ethnic groups, I don't know, but this is the kind of learning we had. I will never forget the kind of things we learned, because to me it all belongs to me. It isn't something that someone says is so; it's mine. I'd want to go hunting, and the guys would know I couldn't get across the stream because it was flooded, but they wouldn't say anything. They'd let me go, and I'd tell them I'd see them later where the rocks are, and they'd say OK knowing all this time I couldn't get through. But they wouldn't tell me that. They'd let me experience it. And I'm grateful to these people for allowing me to have this kind of exploration/learning situation. Secondly, of course, the fact is that maybe I could have gotten across where they couldn't, discovered something different, a method that was new. I think this kind of learning situation is one of the really important things that Indians have today and which could contribute to the society we have today. That is, a learning situation for people, instead of teaching or information-giving.

All these things—the various ways Indian life differed from that in our present society—I didn't learn until after I left the reserve community later on in life. Then I could understand how very differently structured the two communities are. While it didn't have a vertical structure, our community was very highly structured. So highly structured that there wasn't anything that could happen that somebody could almost immediately, in some way, solve, whatever problem arose. Without any given signals or the appearance of any communication whatsoever (there were no telephones), the most complex social action used to happen. If somebody died in that community, nobody ever said we should dig the grave. The grave was dug, the box was made, everything was set up . . . the one who baked pies. Everyone did something in that community, and if you tried to find out who organized it, you couldn't . . .

But it's more than that too. As I see it, organization comes out of a need for immediate order—say, in war. When it develops this way so that people say, "Let's organize," and they get together and create a vertical structure, and place somebody up at the top and then it becomes a power group, and from there on it filters on down until after a while you have somebody running that organization, two or three people or maybe eventually just one, and all the rest of the people get suppressed, pushed down, and held by that very thing they formally sought. You give power to someone and suppress others.

I remember as a child a different kind of organization existing, and I have come to call it now "community consciousness." That community can exist and function and solve all its problems without any kind of signals, like in a school of fish. All of a sudden you see them move; they shift altogether. That is exactly the way most Indian communities function. And yet we have the Department of Indian Affairs coming and telling us we have no organization. The local priest or minister will come and tell us we have to be organized. The Recreation Department will come along and say there's no organization in this community. And when they come it's like shooting a goose in a flock of geese. When you hit him, you disrupt the pattern. So every time you remove a resource person from the community, you disrupt the pattern. You break it up, and they have to reorganize. But in a lot of communities this is very hard to do, and some of them have been too hurt to make it. Indian resource people begin to drop out of sight, and white organizers take over, making it even more difficult for Indian people to function. I know that in one community where there are 740 people (about two-thirds of them children), there are 18 organizations. There are three churches that all have two or three organizations, and there is also a community development officer who has a number of organizations behind him, and they are in such conflict that the community cannot function. It's just sitting there, with people at each other's throats. The people who come in can't understand that if a guy is sitting under a tree and doing nothing but observing the stars or the clouds in the daytime or the birds flying, he is running through a recreational pattern and at the same time learning. These are all parts of a whole. Most Indian people deal with wholeness. It is much different than the way we deal with things where we segment them and deal with them only in parts.

CHARACTERISTICS OF
A NATIVE COMMUNITY:
DISCUSSION PAPER

1. Introduction

After reading Wilfred Pelletier's article, "Childhood in an Indian Village," a number of characteristics common to Native people and their communities during the time Pelletier refers to can be identified.

In groups of 3, discuss the following questions and issues and attempt to develop a group position on each one. Record your responses so that you can share them with the larger group.

2. Discussion Issues

- From your own lists, identify 5 values/concepts about Native people and communities that your group agrees are most important.
- From the group's collective experience, define how the characteristics of Native communities and people articulated in the article differ from those of non-Native communities.
- To what extent do the characteristics Pelletier identifies in his boyhood village remain common in Native communities? What has changed? Why?
- How might the values/beliefs/customs of Native communities in urban areas differ from those of the Native community described in the article? Why?
- If the author of this article walked into the room, what questions would you ask him about his experiences, the changes he has seen, and directions for the future?
- What major changes have occurred in Pelletier's village in his lifetime? How have these affected the people of the community?

THE SHIHIYA CASE STUDY

Purpose

To explore the concept and elements of community-based adult education through the examination of a case study.

Time Required: 1 to 2 hours.

Materials: A copy of The Shihiya Case Study for each student; a chalkboard and flip chart.

Notes on Use

The Shihiya Case Study summarizes the development and operation of an adult education program in a Native community in southern British Columbia. Operating in the 1970s, this program utilized community-based and student-centred principles, and provides a good basis for discussing what community-based adult education is and how it operates.

Procedure

1. Hand out copies of the case study and allow students 10 or 15 minutes to read it. (If pressed for time, this could be assigned the night before.)

2. After everyone has read the article, have the students brainstorm the elements of this program that contributed to its success. Once this is done, ask students to add any other elements to the list that they feel were missing from the program described. List these on a flip chart.

3. Hand out 4 coloured dots to the participants and have

them place their dots by the elements they feel are most critical to a successful Native community-based adult education program.

4. Take the 10 elements with the most dots and arrange these in a circle around a hub labelled 'Native Community-Based Adult Education.' This is the 'development wheel' for Native adult education.

Debriefing

Using the development wheel the students have produced, ask students if a program needs all the elements to be successful. Which are most important? Do each of the elements provide entry points for the development of a good program? How would a chart like this be helpful to adult educators? To community members? Would the same elements be appropriate for all programs in all communities? What might change? Why? For example, would these elements apply to an urban situation? How might they be modified?

Discuss the article itself. The program described operated until 1978. How might a good Native community-based program now be different from the one described? What principles remain the same? How would you apply the principles to your community? Can adult education be used effectively as a tool for community development and social change? How?

NATIVE COMMUNITY-BASED
ADULT EDUCATION:
THE SHIHIYA CASE STUDY

A good Native adult education program has to be owned by the community. It has to be directed by the community, and the community has to know that what comes out at the other end has to be something useful for the community. Because that's the way it will succeed. It has to have that component because adult education is a catalyst for change. It can empower a community to change and develop leaders, develop social workers, develop educators, develop a whole new structure in terms of what's possible . . . . It empowers people to change, and that's very important.
  —Education co-ordinator for the Shihiya Band

The Shihiya band is located in the southern interior of British Columbia. In 1976, the education co-ordinator asked me to work with the Shihiya Band to develop a truly community-based adult education program for his community.

There was little doubt of the need for such a program. Of the 356 band members, over 40% were between the ages of 15 and 34, and of these only 5 had completed high school. In fact, in the 100-year history of the band, fewer than 10 band members had graduated.

By the time I arrived, the band had already secured funding and arranged an affiliation arrangement with the local community college. As the education co-ordinator wrote in 1978:

> It was evident from interaction with the adults that they were not prepared to leave the community to complete grade 10 or 12 . . . . I firmly believed that the program had to be operated in our community and controlled by Native people . . . . The mechanics of the program were that DIA would provide funding, the college would accredit the students' certificates, and the Shihiya Band

administration would administer and control the curriculum and direction of the program. This arrangement allowed for maximum flexibility and the least interference from external agencies.

Based on this arrangement, we began to design a program that would meet the needs of the students involved as well as the community as a whole. We identified six main objectives of the program. It would:

—reflect the realities and needs of the students and their community;

—respect students' cultural and personal integrity;

—provide each student with a positive educational experience regardless of prior success or skill level;

—increase self-confidence and self-respect;

—help students become more confident and able to affect their situation rather than being controlled by it; and

—increase academic skills and provide appropriate credentials.

Two years later, as we looked back over the progress of the program, there was reason to feel we had largely succeeded. In that period, 34 adults, nearly 25% of the entire band membership between 15 and 34, had completed one or both years of the program. Nineteen had received grade 12 diplomas, doubling the number of band members with graduation certificates. More importantly, perhaps, over 90% of all students entering each year completed the program. As the education co-ordinator wrote, "Never before has such a large group in our community stayed together for such a long period of time." Students were able to experience this success in their own community, and almost certainly because it *was* in their community.

This community orientation and group ownership of the program were present from the beginning and were keys to its success. Students were recruited by band members and by word-of-mouth, and by August 1976 we had over 20 students signed up. Individual interviews were held with each student to establish each individual's personal learning and life objectives. What did they want out of the program? Specifics of the program were discussed, and input as to the content, structure, goals, and methods were solicited. Simple assessment tests were administered to establish a baseline for each student and to ensure appropriate placement and materials selection.

Unfortunately, we had no place to house the program. At last, we were told there was only one building available on the reserve—the church. Abandoned for years, it stood behind the band hall in a clearing in the fir trees overgrown with weeds and untended lilac bushes and bounded by a collapsing pole fence. Inside, it was worse. Windows were broken, dust lay everywhere, the walls were cracked and faded, and the old wood floor was grey and water-stained.

So for two weeks, students and instructors (there were 2 assistants) worked to put the place in some order. Outside, the weeds were cut down, the old lawn mowed, and the fence repaired. Inside, the old pews were moved to the back room. The walls got a new coat of white paint. And with a little money from the band, we bought some bright orange carpeting and laid it over the floor. We turned the small balcony into a library, moved a second-hand couch up the steep stairs, and built bookshelves and stocked them with books we bought from a used bookstore. Some of the students with carpentry skills made plywood tables, which we arranged in a circle. We replaced glass and washed the windows, amazed at how much lighter the interior became, and finally covered the tall arched windows with plastic to keep in the heat. Through our efforts, we had transformed an empty and unused building into a warm and comfortable home for our program.

The students were involved in planning the curriculum and structure of the program as well as creating the physical space. Hours were discussed so we could accommodate the greatest number of people; ideas about content were discussed and explained; student goals were further examined; barriers to participation were discussed; and solutions to other problems were sought and implemented (e.g., one student's sister was able to babysit another student's children so she could attend, and rides were arranged).

The program itself was designed to transfer as much responsibility as possible for learning and the operation of the classroom to the learners themselves. Our 5-day schedule, planned and discussed each Monday morning, gave us the opportunity to be flexible in order to accommodate special activities and opportunities while giving learners the chance to have input into the organization of time. Class meetings, where we dealt with problems and complaints, were held on a regular basis, usually every Friday afternoon.

The students were a diverse group; reading levels, for example, ranged from below grade 2.0 to above 12.6. Nonetheless, through a process of dialogue, a stress on co-operative learning while providing for individual needs and differences, utilization of themes that were related to the lives and community of the learners, and stressing concrete learning activities, this diversity was accommodated and led to a sense of a real community with people sharing their strengths and ideas. Adult roles and experiences were acknowledged, and all students could interact at the level they were capable of in discussion and group activities. Their skill levels were not seen as a function of capacity or maturity.

Performance increased as people began to perceive that they were not being classified and limited. Expectations for all students were realistic, but they were also challenging. People who in school had found that teachers expected little from them, and performed accordingly, discovered that they were now expected to work to their potential, and as a general rule they responded.

Worth particular note is the way the program integrated

with and was responsible to the community. Reports were given by the instructional staff as well as students at each monthly band meeting, and community members had opportunities to ask about what we were doing and why. Liaison with the band education co-ordinator was maintained on an almost daily basis. Perhaps most important was the way the resources of the community were utilized, and how the program contributed to the community.

For example, in the construction class (students could elect to take construction or typing), students built a large pole building from plans provided by the Department of Agriculture, doing everything from pouring the footings to building the roof trusses. This building became the band shop and garage. Construction students also completed the basement for a house that would become the daycare centre; they built a chicken coop, including the foundation, insulation, and wiring, which was used by the bookkeeping class to raise chickens.

Bookkeeping itself was a totally community-based and student-centred component. In class, we identified about 8 areas that seemed to be feasible in terms of time, resources and interest, and students chose between these. Those we implemented included cooking, band management, Native courtworker aide, poultry raising, and teacher aide. Cooking included the study of nutrition as well as the preparation of meals for band functions and work with an experienced cook in her kitchen in the community. In band management, students rotated between different band administrators, learning practical bookkeeping as well as other skills. Those volunteering their time to work in this apprentice-style arrangement included the band chief, drug and alcohol counsellor, band manager, bookkeeper, education co-ordinator, lands and estates officer, and band works co-ordinator.

The poultry-raising group read material provided by the British Columbia Department of Agriculture and brought in a local expert to speak on keeping a small poultry flock. He also brought a simple set of books, which we studied to learn the basics of bookkeeping. In addition, we visited a commercial poultry farm and a poultry supply store in nearby communities. After much study, supplies and a flock of 27 chickens were purchased, which involved the entire group negotating a $300 loan. Using the coop built by the construction class, we maintained the chickens (e.g., conducting research into the causes of ailments, treating wounds, cleaning and modifying the coop, buying feed and feeding), collecting and selling the eggs to band members, and keeping an accounting of our sales, feed expenses, and loan payments.

The teacher aide component was a valuable experience involving 15 students over 2 years. It placed these learners in classrooms in the public school (at that time, there was no band school), where there was a number of Native students two days a week for several months. The adult students planned with the teachers, presented lessons, and worked with individual students. The project allowed learners to take an active role in the process so many had left as failures and to critique it first-hand. The schools became less intimidating and the participants became more confident. In the end, the students' evaluations, not to mention their mere presence (this was the first time Native adults had ever been in the school on a regular basis), went a long way toward making the school staff more aware of their responsibility to Native people and helping the Native children in the school feel more comfortable. The ABE students did this through their own activity and participation. They had begun to change their world and themselves.

The 3 students who worked with the Native courtworker helped with paperwork and spent considerable time in court. Reports they wrote indicated an increased understanding of how the courts operate and the circumstances that land a disproportionate number of Native people in jail. One student even stood in for the courtworker, who was unable to be in court, at a hearing. As a result of this experience, the student decided she wanted to become a courtworker.

Math, English and social studies were also taught, of course, all with a Native orientation. Literature by and about Native people was read and discussed; Canadian, British Columbia and local Native history was stressed, along with contemporary issues such as land claims and the Indian Act; and in math, a variety of strands were offered that stressed practical hands-on approaches and applications. In all areas, the experiential, community-based philosophy was emphasized. Elders came to the class on a regular basis to share their knowledge of local history and traditional culture. Interviews were also conducted in their homes, and the results reported to the class or written for the newspaper.

The production of the band newspaper was one of several successful English projects that involved the community as a resource and a beneficiary. Students brainstormed various stories in the community (the number and variety of activities occurring in the community discovered through this exercise surprised many), chose topics to research, conducted interviews and wrote stories, edited each other's stories, sold advertising, typed the material in columns, and laid out the pages. Papers were then printed, collated, and distributed to the community. This project was so successful that several graduates continued putting the paper out for several more years on their own.

Field trips and speakers were also an important part of the program. Playwright George Ryga, author of *The Ecstasy of Rita Joe* and *Indians*, two plays we were studying, came to the school and delivered a very successful reading that drew dozens of people from the nearby white community onto the reserve, many for the first time. Poets Tom Wayman and Susan Musgrave also gave poetry readings to large, receptive audiences. Later they helped students with their own writing.

Field trips played a major role in providing concrete experience to learn from, discuss, and write about. Since a major focus of the program was to help people become more aware of themselves, their world, Native culture, and social problems and solutions, it seemed natural that travel and exposure would figure prominently in the program. Over the 2-year period of the program, trips were taken to Mount Currie (twice), Saskatoon (for the Native American Bilingual/Bicultural Education Conference), Vancouver, southern Alberta, and Nova Scotia, as well as numerous shorter trips to such places as Kamloops, Vernon, and Penticion.

Virtually all these trips were designed to expose students to other Native communities and people, and to show them how Native people all over North America were coping with the same problems and concerns apparent in their own community. In fact, over the 2 years the students spent time in 12 different Native communities from Vancouver to Sydney, Nova Scotia. Each offered something different: in Mount Currie we saw how people can successfully begin and operate their own school system and how this can rejuvenate the entire community; in Nova Scotia we saw how people can hold on to their language and build a strong sense of community despite having small reserves and few resources; in Alberta we saw that big reserves can have big problems, and met some extraordinary people; and in Saskatoon we learned how other Native people across North America are attacking the problem of loss of language and culture. In Vancouver, besides touring a freighter and visiting museums and the University of British Columbia, we toured the Musqueam reserve, visited the Vancouver Native Friendship Centre, ate Native food at the Muk-a-muk, and had a special guided tour of the Native exhibits in the UBC Anthropology Museum.

Our Nova Scotia trip—8 days, including a day and night in Montreal—was certainly our most amibitious trip (although we had tried unsuccessfully to raise enough money to get to Guatemala the year before). Funded through Open House Canada, the Nova Scotia trip took 33 people to Cape Breton Island, where we stayed in 2 Micmac communities and toured the rest of the reserves on the island. Most of the participants had never been in a plane before, let alone travelled to the opposite end of the country. Economic development and cultural projects were explored, and we were all over-whelmed by the hospitality and kindness shown us. For many participants, this trip helped cement a sense of themselves as members of First Nations communities that, while geograph-ically and culturally diverse, had common interests, strengths and backgrounds. Being a Native person took on new and more positive meaning.

Follow-up to these trips was an important aspect of the overall learning experience. Whether writing essays and jour-nal entries for English or studying relevant Native issues, the concrete experiences of the trips resulted in learning that was richer and more significant. On numerous occasions stu-dents acted on their experiences, directly affecting the community. After the first Mount Currie trip, people organ-ized bingo and square dancing and began investigating a band school. This investigation eventually led to the creation of the community school still operating on the reserve. Occa-sionally students acted individually: after visiting the alcohol rehabilitation centre on the Blood Reserve in Alberta, 2 students returned for treatment.

The holistic approach to adult education described here was designed to develop and strengthen both the affective and cognitive aspects of the learners. Indeed, it is my convic-tion that with most adult students the two are necessarily reinforcing and can only occur concurrently. While much of this report has emphasized the social dimensions of the program, the academic outcomes are also important to note. Of the 34 students who completed at least one year, all but 2 received an improved grade standing. Some students were able to advance 2 or even 3 grades in one year, while others took 2 years to complete a single year. This continuous progress model worked well and allowed students to establish their own pace and meet their own objectives. Nineteen students completed grade 12, 7 completed grade 11, 5 grade 10 and 1 grade 9. Records showed an often dramatic increase in skills. Reading scores for students completing both years increased by 2.4 years, and those completing one year showed an average growth of 1.4 years. Of the first 10 who graduated, after being out of the program for one year, one was employed as the band's interim education co-ordinator and playschool instructor, one was working as a full-time teacher aide with the adult education program, another was the band secretary and receptionist, and another was employed as the band carpenter. One student went on to a small business management course in Manitoba, and another graduate became the band's home-school co-ordinator.

This report focusses on a program that terminated almost 15 years ago, and it is difficult to trace all the graduates or the lasting impact the program has had on the community. But it is interesting to note that at a recent meeting with the Shihiya Band council, 3 of the 4 councillors were graduates of the Shihiya Adult Basic Education Program and the fourth was married to a graduate.

—Don Sawyer

MAPPING TRADITIONAL
TERRITORIES

Purpose

To explore participants' knowledge of their aboriginal territories.

Time Required: 1½ to 2 hours.

Materials: Large sheets of paper and marker pens of various colours; a map of the appropriate province or region; maps of the appropriate communities, reserves and traditional territories; a 'key' prepared by the facilitator which includes the information requested in step 2; and traditional stories which mention specific landmarks or locations. *Option:* Find a knowledgable elder to assist.

Notes on Use

You will need to create or identify a 'key' map which can be photocopied and handed out to participants.

The use of traditional stories, whether read or recited by an elder, are optional, but highly recommended. There is power in these ancient stories, and they are important oral documents of 'title' to First Nations peoples' traditional territories.

Procedure

1. Introduce the objectives of the activity and hand out paper and pens.

2. Form participants into groups of 3 or 4 and ask them to

draw maps on flip chart paper which show the traditional territories of their Nations. These maps should show: major geographical features such as rivers and lakes; major contemporary communities; present Native communities; reserves; traditional food and resource utilization sites; tribal boundaries; tribal neighbours; and any places which are mentioned in the traditional stories of their people. *Note:* Participants should attempt to draw a map without any assistance, but it may be necessary to have a map on hand to supply the geographical details, as well as circulating while the maps are being drawn in order to give advice, ideas, hints, and encouragement.

3. Allow the groups to work independently for 20 to 30 minutes, after which the participants should circulate, asking questions and offering suggestions to one another. Make sure that participants focus on sites of traditional resource utilization, especially sites which they, their family, or their community make use of.

4. Have participants present their maps to the large group and explain any details which they have included.

5. Reform into small groups and instruct participants to make additions and corrections to their maps based on the information presented by other groups.

6. When this is finished hand out the 'key' to participants. What is missing from the participants' maps that is on the 'key'? What is missing from the 'key' that is on the participants' maps?

Optional Activities: You may want to read any traditional stories which make reference to specific localities or landmarks, and these can be added to the maps. Or you might invite an elder or elders to tell stories and talk to participants about traditional aboriginal territories.

Debriefing

Attempt to draw out the importance of land and territories to the First Nations in general and the participants in particular. Ask participants if they have a special spot within their traditional territories. Why is this a special spot? Does it have special meaning for other people of your tribe? Is it part of a reserve? Is it public or private land?

If participants did well on their maps, give them positive feedback and try to find out why they knew so much about their traditional lands. If participants did poorly trying to draw these maps on their own, help them to identify why there is a gap in their knowledge, indicating that it is not a personal failing, but a symptom of a system which until very recently systematically ignored Native issues and values politically, socially, and educationally. Emphasize the importance of knowing about their aboriginal territories and their traditional culture as a step toward empowering themselves and First Nations citizens in general.

THE NEWCOMERS

Purpose

This simulation game is designed to help learners better understand what Native people experienced through the loss of control over their lives and territory with the coming of the Europeans. It provides opportunities for discussing such issues as colonialism, ethnocentrism, and the psychological effects of loss of culture.

Time Required: 1½ to 2 hours.

Materials: Eleven poker chips for each Original; jellybeans; jellybeans and chip value charts; enough red and blue tags for Newcomers and Originals respectively (plus some extra blues); role information sheets; $1000 in play money times the number of Newcomers; black cards for the Arbitrator.

Notes on Use

This simulation requires some set up and preparation. Two separate areas are required: a large room with moveable tables and chairs and a large open area for trading, and a second room for assembling and briefing the newcomers. The Arbitrator is key to the game, keeping the pace fast enough to maintain interest and momentum but not so fast that the experience is missed. The Arbitrator also plays the role of the ethnocentric government posing as a neutral observer.

Procedure

1. Divide the participants into 2 groups, the Originals and

the Newcomers, so that $\frac{2}{3}$ are Newcomers and $\frac{1}{3}$ are Originals. Select 1 participant (or the facilitator can play this role) to act as Arbitrator. Originals are given red tags and Newcomers blue tags. Have participants pin these on so they can be seen easily.

2. Set up a room with several tables and desks. Situate the Originals in this room and pass out information sheets. Post the jellybean and chip value charts prominently. Assemble Newcomers in the other area and pass out their information sheets. If a participant is acting as Arbitrator, give him or her the Arbitrator information sheet plus a supply of blue tags and black cards and a jar of jellybeans.

3. After participants have read their instructions, give the Originals 11 poker chips each: 5 white, 3 red, and 3 blue. These are their trade goods. Provide each of the Newcomers with $1,000 of play money in a variety of denominations.

4. Once participants are clear about their roles and objectives, introduce 2 Newcomers into the room. They are to knock and ask permission to enter. This entry is mandatory. They request one table or desk to set up their trading post. Round one of trading begins. After one minute, introduce one more pair of Newcomers; they are to begin trading immediately.

5. After round one, both groups withdraw to their areas to develop strategy. Originals can purchase jellybeans from the Arbitrator, but a small bowl of jellybeans is provided free for the Newcomers by the Arbitrator. Both groups discuss the last round. Allow 2 to 4 minutes. Just before round two, the Arbitrator introduces 2 more Newcomers. This group now selects a spokesperson who will represent their interests and concerns to the Arbitrator. Now that there are 6, the Newcomers, through their spokesperson, have the right to ask the Originals for more space. If they

are refused, they can appeal to the Arbitrator. Then begin round two of trading.

6. Half way into round two, introduce 2 more Newcomers. After the 2 minutes of trading are up, groups reform. Introduce 2 more Newcomers, and as their space becomes more crowded, they can demand more area from the Originals. If there is any resistance, the Newcomers can use their purchased chips to buy space from the Arbitrator. The Originals cannot use their chips to buy land. They are restricted to the tables and area not being used by the Newcomers. Any disputes are referred to the Arbitrator, who may wish to begin using his or her death (black) cards at this point. Before round three begins, introduce the remaining Newcomers into the game.

7. As round three begins, Originals may be more reluctant to trade. The Arbitrator may wish to neutralize the most outspoken members with black cards. These 'dead' players are to sit quietly in chairs set up around the outside of the room. The Arbitrator may also offer Originals a chance to become Newcomers, complete with blue tag and $500, if they turn in their red tags and remaining chips (which are distributed to the Newcomers).

8. After 2 minutes, have players return to their areas. The Arbitrator announces a new rule: Because some of the Originals have not been fully co-operating and some have been threatening to disrupt the game, they will not be able to confer during the 2 minute discussion period. They must remain quiet while the Newcomers have 3 to 4 minutes to confer before round four begins. After discussion, other rules suggested by the Newcomers to overcome Original resistance may be implemented by the Arbitrator.

9. Before round four begins, the Newcomers have the opportunity to buy more area from the Arbitrator with

their chips. They occupy this area, pushing the remaining Originals into the reduced area. The Arbitrator deals with all protests or resistance. If resistance continues, black death cards can be administered. Trading continues for 2 minutes in round four.

10. As before, between rounds the Originals are not allowed to confer with each other. They can speak individually with the Arbitrator, however, who may choose to offer them Newcomer status.

11. Before round five, the final round, begins, Newcomers can buy more land. They may wish to place individual Originals in chalk or string circles from which they cannot move; the remaining area belongs to the Newcomers. They also have the opportunity to propose new rules to the Arbitrator to govern the last trading round.

12. After round five, the Newcomers confer for 5 minutes and make final land purchases. They suggest proposals for dealing with the 'Original Problem.'

Debriefing

Students may need some time to talk about their feelings before the content of the game can be explored. For example, how did Originals feel when they realized they were losing control of the game? When the Arbitrator seemed to favour the Newcomers? When they were pushed into a smaller and smaller area? How did they react? If an Original changed cards, how did the rest of the Originals feel? How did the Originals feel about the Newcomers at first? By the end of the game? How did each group conduct themselves in the game? How else could members of each group have behaved? Why didn't they? Was the game stacked against the Originals? How? (Here the Arbitrator can explain his or her role and actions, and both groups can talk about their instructions.)

Help students connect the activity to historical occur-

rences. Who are the Originals? The Newcomers? How was
the game similar to what really happened? How was it different? Who was the Arbitrator historically? How did the trading
in the game parallel what happened historically? How were
the outcomes of the game similar to historical events? How
might the feelings the Originals and Newcomers had during
the game have been similar to those felt by the real players?
How would they have been different?

What have you learned about Native/non-Native relations? How has this activity affected your views? Why? What
is the real situation for Native people in contemporary society? How might this be rooted in historical occurrences?
What can we do now?

NEWCOMER INSTRUCTIONS

You will be playing a trading game to which only you know the full rules. The object is to acquire as much space in the playing room as possible. You do this by trading play money for the Originals' chips. The chips you acquire will allow your group to purchase more area, so bargain as hard as you can, especially in the early rounds before the real value of the chips is later realized. Later on you will have the chance to develop strategies and guidelines to regulate the game. Regard these as opportunities to benefit as much as possible from the game.

ORIGINAL INSTRUCTIONS

You are a member of a group that occupies the trading room. You will be participating in a trading game with the Newcomers. You are hospitable and generous, the room's plenty big, and the game will be interesting. It should be fun. You have been given an assortment of chips, which you can trade with the Newcomers for their money. The money you acquire will allow you to buy jellybeans during the discussion periods. See the chart for how much money it will take to buy one bean. Have fun.

ARBITRATOR INSTRUCTIONS

You are the key to this game. Your task is to secretly assist the Newcomers in their acquisition of area in the trading room. To do this you should almost always find in favour of the Newcomers if there is an appeal or protest and you should do everything possible to help as they take over more tables and territory. After all, you are one of them, and anyway, their numbers are increasing and they need the area.

You have four special powers. (1) You can unilaterally decide any disputes or requests. (2) You can sell area to the

Newcomers for chips after the second round. How many chips you require for what area is up to you, but the area purchased should roughly correspond to the total value of the chips (100 times the number of Originals) in the game. (3) You can hand out black 'death' cards to Originals. Use this tactic to reduce the group size and neutralize trouble makers. The chips of black carded Originals are distributed among the Newcomers. (4) You can offer Newcomer status to Originals by having them give up their red card for a blue one. Their chips are redistributed among the Newcomers. This offer can be made to individuals after the third round, especially those creating problems.

JELLYBEAN CHART

$100 = 1 jellybean (any colour)
$200 = 3 jellybeans
$300 = 5 jellybeans
$500 = 10 jellybeans

CHIP POINT CHART

White = 5 points
Red = 10 points
Blue = 15 points

BEHAVIOURS THAT IMPEDE NATIVE/NON-NATIVE RELATIONSHIPS

Purpose

To explore some of the behaviours that impede Native/non-Native relationships, and to identify and discuss behaviours that facilitate good Native/non-Native relationships.

Time Required: 1 hour.

Materials: Copy of 'Behaviours That Impede Good Relationships' sheet for each student; chart paper, felt pens, paper, pencils.

Notes on Use

The list of impeding behaviours identified here was assembled by a group of Native and non-Native educators and is in no way comprehensive or definitive. Be prepared to explain and discuss the items and assure participants that they are for reflection and discussion, and cannot be applied to all situations or people, be they Native or non-Native. For further information on Native and non-Native communication patterns, see Ron and Suzanne Scollon's book, *Narrative Literacy and Face and Interethnic Communication* (Norwood, New Jersey: Ablex Publishing). Depending on the experience of students and the time available, you may wish to skip steps 1 and 2 and begin directly with step 3.

Procedure

1. Instruct students to think of one or more unsuccessful Native/non-Native interactions they have witnessed or with which they have been involved. These situations could be from television or movies, or ones which they have overheard or experienced themselves. Have them recall the incidents in detail.

2. Ask students to make 2 columns on a sheet of paper, labelling one 'Native' and the other 'Non-Native.' In each column, students should list the differing behaviours that seemed to get in the way of understanding between Native and non-Native people. Instruct them to be as specific as possible.

3. Hand out copies of 'Behaviours That Impede Good Relationships' to students. Have them study the list of 10 items for each group and circle 3 *in each category* that they feel, based on their experience, most often get in the way of good Native/non-Native communications.

4. Divide participants into groups of about 4, combining Natives and non-Natives if possible, and have them try to reach agreement on which 3 behaviours in each category are the biggest impediments to good relations. Encourage them to draw on their own experiences to explain their choices.

5. Reform the larger group and ask students to share the results of their discussions. Note those behaviours that were most identified as impeding good relationships on a flip chart or an overhead. This can be done based on group reports or individual selections. Discuss these behaviours and why they are common and harmful to good relationships, asking students to share their own experiences.

6. Have the groups meet once more to generate a list of 5 behaviours that *facilitate* good relationships. Instruct each

group to list these on a flip chart and post them on the wall, then ask each group to explain the behaviours they have identified and why they chose them.

Debriefing

Have students experienced unsuccessful Native/non-Native interactions? What were the results?

How was the list you generated based on your own experience similar to or different from the list handed out? What would you add to those listed? Subtract?

What breakdowns between cultural groups have you seen take place? Why are the impeding behaviours noted so difficult to change? Which are culturally rooted?

BEHAVIOURS THAT IMPEDE
GOOD RELATIONSHIPS

Behaviours of Some Non-Natives

1. Condescension: looking down on the actions of others.
2. Offering help when not needed or wanted.
3. Ethnocentricity: being unaware of culturally-based communication and behaviour patterns.
4. Showing intolerance for Native behaviours and/or values that differ from their own.
5. Overly-easy expressions of friendship and acceptance.
6. Aggressiveness and verbal domination.
7. Stereotyping: assuming all Natives are alike.
8. Making comments that reflect an ignorance of Native culture and issues.
9. Asking too many questions.
10. Interrupting when the other person is speaking.

Behaviours of Some Natives

1. Pushing non-Natives into a defensive posture.
2. Talking off-topic.
3. In-group joking about non-Natives.
4. Letting non-Natives dominate conversation and draw conclusions without Native intervention.
5. Passivity or withdrawal.
6. Stereotyping: assuming all non-Natives are alike.
7. Misdirecting anger.

8. Confrontation too early, too harshly.

9. Rejection of honest gestures of kindness, acceptance and friendship.

10. Slow to take turn in conversation.

COMMUNITY FUTURES

Purpose

To encourage participants to visualize the future of their community, (and by implication, Native communities in Canada), and to think about their role in bringing that vision about.

Time Required: 1¾ hours.

Materials: Large sheets of paper for each small group (newspaper roll ends or several sheets of flip chart paper joined together), markers, paint or crayons.

Notes on Use

While this activity is primarily designed to be used with First Nations students, it can also be used with other groups or sub-groups which share a common community.

Procedure

1. Ask participants to think of their community in 10 years time. Have them spend some time individually thinking of the future that they *hope* for their community. What sort of services would there be? What educational and economic opportunities would they like to see exist? How would people spend their leisure time? What medical, spiritual and cultural institutions would there be? How would they be governed?

2. Have participants form groups of 4 or 5. Have each group first discuss, and then pictorially portray, their future community. This portrayal should be a sort of annotated,

pictorial map/mural of the community. Encourage creativity and originality. Symbols rather than words should be used wherever possible. This is not an exercise of artistic ability, but a process which assists people to articulate their hopes and dreams for their community.

3. After 30 to 35 minutes have participants reform into the large group and briefly explain their drawings to the group. Post the drawings on the wall and allow viewing time.

4. Ask participants to note similarities between the drawings of the different groups. Note especially what sort of services are offered in the community. What are the educational and economic opportunities? How are they governed? Is there Native self-government yet?

5. Ask participants to identify potential obstacles which might prevent their community from developing into the community of their drawing. (List these on flip chart.) Which of these are external and which are internal obstacles?

6. Have participants reform small groups and share what they as individuals can do to overcome the obstacles and help bring about the healthy community of their drawing. Ask participants to share what they *will* do to help bring about their healthy community.

7. Ask participants what they think will be the state of Native peoples in Canada in 10 years time. Have the same small groups discuss this topic. They may want to focus on both the institutions of Native communities as well as the state of Native peoples on a more personal and emotional level.

8. As a final activity, have participants do a 10 minute quickwrite about their hopes and expectations for Native people in Canada. You may have to explain what a quickwrite is.

Debriefing

During all phases of this activity, encourage participants to articulate what makes their community different from mainstream Canadian communities, and what gives their community a Native identity. Request that students focus on personal and emotive factors rather than formal institutions and structures.